UNLOCKING THE DOORS OF YOUR HEART

A New Look at Love

Russell M. Abata, C.SS.R., S.T.D.

LIGUORI
PUBLICATIONS

One Liguori Drive
Liguori, Missouri 63057
(314) 464-2500

Imprimi Potest:
John F. Dowd, C.SS.R.
Provincial, St. Louis Province
Redemptorist Fathers

Imprimatur:
+ Edward J. O'Donnell
Vicar General, Archdiocese of St. Louis

ISBN 0-89243-204-7
Library of Congress Catalog Card Number: 83-83442

Table of Contents

"He [God] knows the secrets of the heart" (Psalm 44:22).

This book is for those who desire to learn the secrets of love by opening the doors of their hearts.

Introduction

Many reasons have prompted me to write this book on love.
Here are but two of them.

My first purpose is to clarify the issues in the ongoing war
between love and sex.

Those on the side of love insist that true freedom must be
based on reason and rules. They maintain that sex without love
and commitment is wrong. It is a horrible mutilation of what
should be a sublime experience.

Those on the other side insist that as long as no one gets hurt
people should be free to do as they please. They maintain that
pleasure is a sufficient motive for having sex. Love and commitment are not required.

The forces in favor of unrestricted sex have made such
advances that it has been considered old-fashioned to speak of
sexual morality. But, of late, the situation has changed somewhat. Some have come to recognize the inevitable emptiness of
sex without love. Others have had to face the horror of a disease
called herpes. This has forced them to take a closer look at
freedom without a concern for consequences.

I have written this book not to judge or condemn anyone but
to present a full picture of love. It is hoped that these pages will
place you in a better position to decide for yourself which side
makes more sense.

My second and more important purpose for writing this book is to share with you something tremendously important to me. As an artist who has seen a beautiful sight wants to share it with others, I want to share with you some of the beautiful truths I have learned about love. I think they can make a difference in your life. I have seen so many die of thirst because they have not drunk from the living waters of the heart. They have this refreshing water within them, but it is locked away and untouchable. It is worth every effort to try to free this living flow of life and love.

I consider my sharing with you in this book an act of love. I hope you look on it the same way.

Russell M. Abata, C.SS.R.

(Note: Each chapter in this book closes with examples, which emphasize the point being made, and with a series of questions intended for review of the material covered.)

1

The Moving Ways of Love

We may look at love in different ways. One way is to see it as establishing a kind of rhythm between one person and another. It is an experience in moving and, at the same time, a moving experience.

Think about that a moment.

You see and hear someone who appeals to you. You say to yourself, "I like her." "I like him."

What are you saying?

You are saying that from what you see and what you hear you want to get closer to that person. Some kind of magnet is drawing you to her or to him.

Maybe it is the magnet of your sense of touch and sexuality.

Maybe it is the magnet of your feelings.

Maybe it is the magnet of your mind.

Whatever it is, you want a touch, feeling, or mind contact with that other person. You want to draw her or him into your touch, feelings, or mind.

You desire a close personal relationship with the other. You want that person to move into your personality, and you want to move into his or hers.

How do you bring this about?

It can be accomplished through any and all of the doors of your heart. Some of these doors are outer, others are inner. They are your senses, appetites, feelings, mind, and will. Each one leads into your innermost self.

What opens these doors?

Your senses are easily opened by what you see, feel, and touch. If what they sense is attractive, they automatically assume goodness. If what they sense is unattractive, they show no further interest.

Your appetites open and close themselves following the lead of your senses.

Your feelings are also highly influenced by your senses. They open wide to what is pleasurable.

Your mind relies on your senses for its information, but it investigates their reports and only opens up to what is authentic. It searches for fact, not fabrication.

Your will opens up to goodness.

We will take a more detailed look at all of these entrances and exits of your personality.

Your
Senses

Your eyes, ears, and touch are the outside doors of your personality. They let another into you.

Your eyes snap a picture of the outline and details of another's face and figure. Your optical nerves relay this picture to your brain. In a very real way, then, you have the other within you.

Your ears pick up the sound of another. As they hear words being cleverly or clumsily put together, they help you to judge the intelligence or lack of intelligence of the other. They give a sound dimension to the picture provided by your eyes.

Your touch allows you to make an immediate contact with another. Since there is no space between the other and your touch, your touch contact makes even more real the picture furnished by your eyes and ears. Your touch lets the other vibrate and melt into you.

If the reports of your senses are favorable, you want to keep them inside of you even after sense contact has been broken. You return to the impressions the other has made to keep them as long as possible. You hope that you, too, have made a deep, favorable impression. If the other looks, listens, and touches you intensely, you know you have. You have entered the outside doors of the other's being.

Your Appetites

When another has made a favorable impression on your senses, your appetite or instinct for survival is activated. You realize you do not have to be alone. You have found someone you would like as a helpmate.

If the helpmate is a member of the opposite sex, a further instinct or appetite goes to work. You have begun to open your being to receive another or to exit from yourself sexually. You have powerful forces at work inside of you that want you to go out of yourself to the other. You do not want to stay within the walls of yourself. You want to be in the other's being as you were in the womb of your mother.

When this happens, so much biology and chemistry are let loose within you that your whole being is affected. It almost seems to be happening on its own, and you are the excited spectator. You seem to be outside of yourself, wanting to be completely in the other. Of course, what your biology and chemistry are trying to accomplish is to join you to the other so that the life-giving components of your beings can come together and bring forth a new being. This new being would magically unite the two of you in a permanent way. The child would be the two of you.

With all of this and more going on when your sexuality is activated, it is little wonder that sex has such an appeal. Unfortunately, the appeal and pleasure of sex can so steal the scene that the real purpose of entering more deeply into another's personality, not just his or her body, is overlooked. As a result, when the biological and chemical fireworks are spent, the show can be over and the two might not be any closer than before. Some can even go their respective ways as if nothing really important has happened.

Couples who are sexually mature do not make the above mistakes. In many ways they have taken a giant step into each other's beings, and their act of sex is a joyful, as well as a pleasurable, expression of their oneness. Their sexual exchange is an exterior, symbolic expression of deeper and more-difficult-to-express onenesses.

Your Feelings

Up to this point, another's entrance into your personality and your entrance into his or hers is not that deep. It can seem deep because it is intense, but being intense and deep are not the same.

Deeply personal relationships come into being when you receive another into your feelings and another receives you into his or her feelings.

And what are your feelings? That might seem like a foolish question to ask. Everyone knows what feelings are. You feel glad or you feel sad.

Yes, everyone experiences feelings, but how are they described?

Your feelings are another force or part of you that appraise — in a more total way — the people or person your senses have invited into your innermost self. They are concerned with more than looks and sex appeal; they want to know what pleasure the other can give. Is he or she pleasant or boring, intelligent or shallow, selfless or selfish?

As they perceive how pleasing or displeasing another is, your feelings respond favorably or unfavorably. It is almost as if your feelings are a neutral liquid inside of you — like water. What you add to the water will determine how it will taste. What your senses present to your feelings determines their reaction. If the person presented is pleasing, your feelings become cheerful and confident. If the person is ugly or displeasing, your feelings become fearful, angry, and even desperate.

This is how your feelings work.

They are precious.

How you feel about someone will probably set the pace of your whole day. If the person is pleasing, you want to fill every possible moment with thoughts of him or her. Even when there is a physical distance between you, knowing how deeply he or she feels about you, there is no real separation. You can feel the other inside of you, or you can feel yourself inside the other. Not even the distractions of absorbing activities can keep you apart. For awhile they can take away your awareness of the other, but that is all. A free moment, a glance at a picture or the touch of a keepsake — these all return the magic of the other's presence.

Your Mind

Having entered through your senses, been reviewed by your appetites and feelings, the object of your affections must now pose before the camera of your brain — your imagination. Only after this image-making process is completed can the other person enter your mind. With the aid of these many-angled pictures your mind will then appraise the other in terms of authentic worth or goodness.

"Is this other person's goodness real or counterfeit? Does he or she possess real intelligence, independence, and ability to cope with life or not?"

If your mind is not unduly influenced by your appetites and feelings, it will give you an honest judgment about the other. This judgment may be doubtful because of conflicting elements reported by your senses and imagination, or it may be certain.

If your mind's judgment is unfavorable but your appetites and feelings do not want to hear this, it may take a considerable amount of time before the truth of your mind hits home and you can act on it.

If the judgment is favorable — the other is all that he or she appears to be and more — your mind delights in the fact. And if you know the other thinks highly of you, you are enriched many times over. It is like having a double dwelling place. Your mind cannot wait to pass on its judgment to your will.

Your Will

The deepest capacity of your personality is your will.

Because they are moved and controlled by their feelings, many persons speak of them as their "heart." They refer to a "change of heart," for example, as a change of mind, affections, loyalties, etc. True, the heart represents the very core of their being, revealing their inmost thoughts and feelings. But there is another force within them that is too often ignored. That force is their will, their free will.

How is the will described?

Your will is a power, an inner drive that searches out goodness. If it is developed and free, it listens to what your senses, appetites, feelings, and mind reveal. It views their reports in terms of goodness. It tells you whether another is good and whether that other is good for you. If that goodness is sufficient to win your will's approval, you cannot wait to let him or her into the core of your being.

Of course, this choice of alternatives and decision to act is not as simple as it appears on paper. Your senses, appetites, and feelings can be so powerful that they force your mind to see only what they want it to see. Either your will is not consulted or it is fed falsified information that is judged as good because it appears to be good. In such cases, neither your mind nor your will is able to render an unbiased judgment and choice. Someone may be looked on favorably and let into your being who really is not good or is not good for you. It may take a long time for the mistake to be discovered and corrected.

But when your will is strong enough to be free and you have found another who is truly good, you have found a pearl of great price. And if the other looks on you in the same way, that pearl is yours. You cling to the other with all your will, with all your heart, with all your being. You hold open for him or her the rooms inside of you reserved for those who are solidly good.

What Love Does to You

Has the presentation of all these different ways of moving into another and having another move into you worn you out? Trying to picture them in your mind can be tiring, but your efforts here can result in a rewarding experience. Some of the effects of the experience are automatic. Some are not. All of them together should give you a full picture of solid love.

Human love is more than entering another's senses and exciting his or her sexual appetite. It is capable of much more —

the other becomes present in your very being even though absent from your physical senses.

The other is present in your feelings. You are present in his or her feelings.

The other is present in your mind. You both continually think about each other.

If the other is present in your will, nothing can remove him or her.

There is no loneliness. It may seem to others that you are a lonely piece of driftwood on an ocean shore, but you are a beehive of activity. A busy switchboard is at work within you trying to handle all the calls and connections coming from your senses, appetites, feelings, mind, and will. The other is where you are. You are where the other is. Your physical senses may be helpless against the barriers of distance or time, but not the other connecting powers within you.

As you walk along the shore of love, you gather the seashells and bright colored stones discovered by love's entrance through the doors of your "heart." In spirit, you share them with your loved one. You can't wait to share them with him or her in person.

Once residence has been firmly established — the other is in you and you are in the other — not only does loneliness disappear but some very beautiful, positive things begin to happen.

If you are experiencing another in an "in love" way, you are caught up in breathtaking adventure. The pleasures of such an experience are poetry itself. You find yourself thinking in rhyme. And you begin to express your love in rhapsodic words. Morning, noon, and night the other surfaces like a cork to the top of your thoughts and being.

You can hardly think of anyone else.

You hardly think of yourself.

The other is always there awaiting your attention.

If you have passed beyond an "in love" experience to a commited sexual love, you find a similar but different kind of magic at work. You are riding down the rapids of a river that carries you into the deep, refreshing pool of love. You are experiencing joy.

In a quiet, at-home way, your whole being belongs to the other. There is no worry, no hurry. A look or a touch is as stimulating as a sexual experience. In some ways, being symbols and not driven by biology or chemistry, these simple expressions of love signify more than overt sexuality and intense feelings. Of course, the perfect combination would be for the "in love" experience to have the more lasting, loving experience as its foundation and for the loving experience to use whatever of the "in love" experience is appropriate for the circumstances.

There is nothing else in life quite like the rhythmic adventure of love as described in this chapter.

Summary

The moving ways of love have been described in this chapter. It enters into your life through the doors of your "heart," your inner being. These doors are called your senses, appetites, feelings, mind, and will. And when each of these plays its part to perfection, you experience the most moving experience in your life.

Cathy

Cathy is a married woman in her late thirties. She has three children.

Ten years ago when Cathy met Bill she considered herself a very lucky person. Bill was all that she was not. He was sure of himself. He would solve her doubts with simple answers or a nod of the head. He was like a castle where she could run when she was afraid.

But, as time passed, Cathy realized that something was wrong. Their sex life was satisfactory, but every effort she made to enter into Bill's personality was rebuffed. She tried to get into his feelings, but they were surrounded by walls. She tried to find an entrance into his mind, but he seemed to resent her silly talking.

She was hurt.

She was angry.

She resolved not to care, and she kept her resolution. Unfortunately, everything went dead inside of her. Exteriorly she looked fine, but interiorly she was alone and scared. Only the thought of the children kept her from running away from it all.

It is obvious that Cathy is a prisoner in her own home. She does escape on occasion — to buy nice things to distract her, but they do not free her. When her shopping is over, she returns to herself and the confinement of her locked heart.

Tony

A social worker in his early forties, Tony has seen too much of the ugly side of life. He has not thought seriously of marriage, mainly because of his past experiences with girls. Some of them seemed nice at first, but after dating them a while he always came away disappointed — until he met Sue.

What was it about Sue that changed Tony's mind about serious relationships?

Tony was not sure. He only knew that when he was with her, he was completely relaxed. She let him into her life so graciously — by revealing her feelings and inner being — that she became a part of him almost before he realized it. And he automatically opened the doors of his heart to her.

It was that simple. He did not have to analyze it. "I have never been more close to and aware of another, and yet I have never been more aware of myself. Sue has become a part of me, but she is not a burden. I do not mind hearing her problems. Maybe it is because she does not try to make them my problems. I don't understand it, but I like it. I want more of it. I want to gaze at, be with, and share everything with this walking, talking flower of goodness."

Sue has so unlocked Tony's heart that she can enter and steal what she wants. But, of course, this is not stealing. Everything in him is hers.

Questions

1. Are you surprised at the number of ways that love has for making you one with another? Has this first chapter given you some indication of how to put these ideas into practice?

2. To help you unlock your heart in the ways indicated in this chapter, answer the following questions about your own way of loving.

(a) How do you personally let another into your life or yourself into another's life? Is this only through your senses or appetites? Does this person's absence make your heart grow fonder, or does a prolonged absence cause you to forget him or her?

(b) Do you allow another into your feelings? Do your feelings run deep, or are they only surface? Are you afraid to feel deeply? Does it hurt you too much to feel deeply? Have you been hurt before?

(c) Do you give another free access into your mind, or are you afraid to let another in? Do you think of another often? Do you picture this person as he or she actually is, or has your imagination touched it up to some degree? Do you think this other person pictures you as you actually are?

(d) Have you ever allowed another into the deep recesses of your will, or is your will practically inactive because your appetites or feelings are in control of you? Do you want this person to come into your heart because you want to lean on him or her or because you recognize and want to share his or her goodness? Is the other's goodness solid enough to challenge you into wanting to enter deeply into the mystery of his or her personality? Does it seem from where you are now that it will take an eternity to comprehend and enjoy this person fully?

3. What do you think of this idea of love as an experience in moving? Have you experienced love that way? Is it an idea that appeals to you?

4. What do you think of Cathy and her situation? Remembering Cathy's insecurities, what realistic suggestions would you give her?

5. How do you feel about Tony? Do you feel he is caught up in an "in love" experience or in something more substantial?

Attraction: Key to the Doors of Your Heart

If you find that some doors of your heart or those of another's are locked, how can they be unlocked? If some of them have never been opened, what will open them?

Obviously, these are crucial questions about love that need simple, workable answers. This chapter will aid you in your search.

Meaning of Attraction

Although it might sound so simple that it makes you smile to hear it, the doors of your heart swing open to attraction. Your senses, appetites, feelings, mind, and will need a stimulus to start them working. It can be something that is appealing or repulsive. If it is appealing, they go after it. The more attractive it is, the more they move toward it. If it is repulsive, they want to get you away from it as fast as possible. They slam their doors shut on it. If it is something hurtful they have experienced before, they lock their doors.

We will see the importance of all of this as we move along. For now, it can be helpful to point out an important truth about attraction: Whoever does the attracting is the active person. He or she is the magnet. The person attracted is passive.

So, when you love someone, the other is the magnet drawing you. You are not drawing him or her. (Only when you are loved in return do you become the magnet.) Actually, this is the opposite of what the words indicate. Loving is active. Being loved is passive. In reality, loving another, you are passive. Being loved, you are active. Confusing, isn't it?

"What," you may ask, "is so enlightening about all of this? What difference does it make who is active and who is passive?"

It makes a world of difference. Most people want to be loved. Their understanding is that they do not have to do anything to make it happen. They are the passive, receiving ones. They expect someone to come and fill them, not receive from them. So they wait and wait and wait for it to happen. They do nothing to make it happen. When it does not happen, they can become so bitter that their bitterness makes them even less attractive.

Ways of Attracting

So, if you want to be loved, *you* need to be attractive.

"That is the difficulty," you complain. "I am not attractive."

That is not true. You might not be physically stunning, but that is not the only way to be attractive. That is the most popular way, but it is only the beginning. As we have seen, this only opens the front door of another's appetites; the other doors remain unopened. You would be wise, even if you are physically attractive, to concentrate more on the other's feelings, mind, and will. These forms of attraction open the doors leading to another's inner self. Then you may become a permanent resident instead of a visiting guest.

So, there are many ways of being attractive. It is up to each person to choose the way or ways best suited for him or her. The statement "I am not attractive" is only a statement. It probably is more of a prejudice than a fact. Even if it is a fact, a present fact, it can change. You can work at being attractive. How many times have you heard someone say, "I do not know what that woman has, but after a few minutes in the company of others she outshines women who are prettier. Others look pretty, but she radiates beauty. She has an intangible flow about her that outweighs her physical flaws."

What is her secret? Can you learn anything from her?

In seeking to be attractive you have at your service what nature has given you and what you can do to enhance nature. Both nature and art are available to everyone, and you should use them to make yourself attractive. They should work together.

A few words of caution might be helpful here.

Try not to confuse being natural with being plain or neglecting to use what nature has given you. No, what is natural can be anything but plain, and getting in touch with what is natural can take a great deal of work.

As to plainness, if you are really in touch with yourself, your face will show it. Your eyes will be alive. Your skin, voice, and manner will communicate what is happening within you. All the makeup in the world could not bring out what you are expressing naturally. It can help, but it cannot compare to what is natural.

As to using what nature has given you, it is not always easy to have your inner forces flow freely and surface naturally. There can be so many barriers to overcome.

So, being natural is being alive in yourself and to yourself. It is the best way to be attractive. Any skillful application of art to nature will make you more attractive. But it will be an addition, not a substitution.

We will see this more clearly as we consider how you become attractive through the doors of your personality.

Attracting Another's Senses

In your efforts to make yourself attractive, besides being in touch with your internal nature, it will help to observe the world of external nature that surrounds you. God made the world of nature for human beings, so he clothed it with fascinating features.

What is it in nature that attracts your eyes? When you see a field of wild flowers, why do you marvel at their beauty? Obviously, it is the splashes of color that have caught your eyes.

What is it in nature that appeals to your ears? Isn't it soothing to hear the rhythmic roll of ocean waves running their fingers on the keyboard of the shore?

What in nature is more appealing to your touch than the soft, velvet petals of a rose?

All of these experiences are meant by nature to appeal to your senses. You need only become aware of and show your personal interest for them to take effect.

Have these or other examples of nature that appeal to you given you any ideas on how to attract another by way of his or her senses? Can you work with combinations of light and color to catch another's eyes? Can you improve the sound of your voice by relaxing, slowing down, and breathing deeply? Can you acquire a softness of touch by reacting more peacefully to the circumstances or people that tense and harden your features?

This is an area where your personal attention will produce good results. If your goal is to be attractive — not sensational — you will succeed. The important point is that you work at it. You never know when someone passing by will find in you what he or she has been looking for.

Attracting Another's Appetites

We will restrict our consideration here to your instinct or appetite for sex.

This is a very important but delicate area of attraction. We do not want to minimize or exaggerate the uniting power of sex.

To begin with, we want to establish that sex is a valid form of attraction. God made it so. Unfortunately, some religious teachers have treated sex as if God had made a mistake when he entrusted sex to human beings. They do not say so outright, but their attitude implies it.

This is not the way it should be. Males and females were meant to attract each other sexually. To do this, they must be sexually appealing to each other.

So, we must ask the delicate question: How much sexual exposure is modest and moral?

There is no fixed answer to this question. So much depends on the times. A great deal also depends on circumstances.

As to the times, it would shock many of today's religious-minded people to read about the amount of exposure that was considered modest and moral by eighteenth-century theologians.

As to circumstances, certainly presence on a beach or the heat of a summer's day allows much more exposure than other occasions.

Perhaps the best answer to this question of how much sexual exposure for attracting another is modest and moral is to say that it is left to the good taste of the times and circumstances. Chastity is a moral virtue. It is an attitude that avoids the extremes of too little or too much exposure. It is a decision that should be based on common sense and the acceptable fashions of the time or circumstances.

(For further information about sexual attraction and the morality of sexual actions, consult my book *Sexual Morality*, published by Liguori Publications, One Liguori Drive, Liguori, Missouri 63057.)

Attracting Another's Feelings

It is fairly simple to attract the senses and appetites, as we have just seen; but is it just as easy to appeal to another's feelings or emotions?

The key to everyone's feelings is that they open to what is pleasing or pleasurable. Now perhaps you are thinking to yourself: "Then to be attractive all I have to do is to be pleasant and do pleasing things for another. That is easy enough."

In dealing with many people, it is just that simple. They are so pleased that another wants to please them that they open their doors quite readily to such treatment. However, in today's complex world, it is not always so easy to gain an entrance into another's feelings. Consider the following cases.

Some people have so little contact with their feelings that they really don't know what will please them. How are you to know this? Will you try everything and be willing to keep on trying when nothing seems to work?

Others have a number of infantile or juvenile feelings that need satisfying before they can proceed to outgoing feelings. Will you be capable of acting like a part-time mother or father to them?

Still others — without realizing it — appear to want rejection rather than acceptance. What will you do? Will you become silent and stop trying? That would only further convince them that they are not worth much; and yet, if you keep trying, you yourself will be rejected. Can you handle that?

So, there are problems to be faced in this complicated area. Fortunately, there is a method for solving them.

A safe way to penetrate another's feelings is to find, not force, an entrance.

To shower another with gifts, compliments, and attention is forcing the other to open up his or her feelings. Such an overwhelming display of caring might work for a time, but after a while it loses its effectiveness. To find the existing openings in another's feelings and to enter through them is a more difficult but preferable way.

How is this done?

The most important step is to look and listen for feelings. What is the person really feeling? Let's call her Lois. Is she lonely? If so, is it because she is afraid she cannot cope with her life? Or is it because she is in need of someone to give her some self-esteem?

There is a difference between the two, and it is important to realize it.

Loneliness is a feeling that there is no one around, even when people are around. That may sound strange, but what such persons' feelings are saying is that there is no one there for them. No one really cares. This confuses their friends. They protest that they care. Why, then, does it not take away the others' feelings of loneliness?

It is important, therefore, to see whether our Lois feels lonely because she cannot cope or because she is empty of self-esteem. If she is afraid she cannot cope and you praise her because you want to boost her self-esteem, you only make matters worse. You are telling her she can do what she feels she cannot do. Your words and presence are useless. You do not understand; and, because you do not, you make her feel more lonely, stupid, and desperate. If you detect the real cause of her loneliness and help her with that, she will, perhaps reluctantly, open the doors of her feelings.

The important tool for opening another's feelings is to use your own feelings. Your intellect is not very helpful here. It is much too tall to enter the smaller openings provided by feelings.

This, of course, will demand a healthy amount of patience on your part. Those openings have been stubbornly and, at times, cleverly blocked as a means of protection. To open them, you may have to be just as stubborn and clever as the other person.

Attracting Another's Mind

It may sound strange to speak of attracting another's mind, but it is a realistic manner of loving. Animals, for example, can only let you into their senses, their appetite for survival, and their feelings. They have no other rooms within them. Human beings do. They have the spacious rooms of their spiritual side. The mind is one of them. If another lets you into his or her mind, you have entered deeply into his or her personality. So, it is not strange to speak in this way. It is different because most do not approach it directly, but that does not make it less valid.

Now, what attracts the mind depends on the development of the person.

Persons who have not reached a level of development higher than their senses, appetites, and feelings find that their minds are controlled by these forces. To satisfy them is their only purpose in life. Their minds are searchlights in pursuit of pleasure and avoidance of pain. But the minds of persons who have developed beyond this domination are free to function on their own. They give their reports on the basis of what is real or true and what is not.

In seeking to attract another's mind, you therefore have to

know the kind of mind with which you are dealing. If you try to attract by means of truth and reality a mind imprisoned by senses, appetites, and feelings, you will not succeed. If you try to attract a mature mind with only pleasures and the avoidance of pain, you will not succeed.

Obviously, then, if you have a choice and the ability to appreciate it, it is better to enter into the mind of someone who is not dominated by his or her senses, appetites, and feelings. And that is the kind of mind we will consider here.

To attract the minds of mature persons you have to be interested in relationships. Mature men and women seek to find out how things are related. They ask, ''Why is this happening? What purpose does that serve?'' Their minds presuppose that everything has a purpose and everyone has a goal. They assume that another mind has arranged matters in this way.

Now, if you can show another how things are related, you excite that person's mind. (Let's call him Lewis.) He is excited over what he is learning from you, and he is delighted because he knows you will understand the things he has learned and wants to share. No matter what kind of knowledge the two of you are sharing, your minds are big enough for each to enter comfortably and to be at home there.

Certainly, then, the more your sharings deal with truths about human beings and human ways, the more gratifying they are. And if these discoveries can make clearer to you the deep mysteries of life, love, and God, you are enraptured by them.

But how do you do this?

Actually, it is done in much the same way as when you — as a child — matched one block with another. As a mature person, you arrive at further truth by matching one object with another. You look at a girl's long hair and compare it to a waterfall. You say, ''Her hair reminds me of water cascading over a fall.'' And the other says, "That is true. Why didn't I think of that? Why don't I think that way? That is exciting."

You *can* think that way if you work at it.

It is a sure way into another's mind.

Attracting Another's Will

As the way of attracting another's mind is determined by whether that person is controlled or not controlled by his or her senses, appetites, and feelings, so it is with the will.

If the other's will is controlled only by what appeals to the senses, appetites, and feelings, it will be difficult to enter; and, even if you succeed in reaching it, you really have not gained very much. If something more pleasurable presents itself or something too painful appears on the scene, you will be ignored or evicted.

Let's suppose that you want to attract and help the dominated will of such a person. How would you go about it?

You know right off that those whose wills are so dominated cannot be attracted by what is reasonable and good. So, it makes no sense to tell them the good things they should do for themselves. They are basically interested in gaining pleasure and avoiding pain. If you can help them with either, they may or they may not listen. Here perhaps it would be best to use the tactics described on pages 31 and 32.

As much as it is possible, then, you should let an individual follow his or her own lead. Stay close by, but do not interfere. Encouraged by your trust, the other will eventually begin to see the importance of the will in making life's decisions.

This takes a great deal of patience. But despite evident embarrassment and even exasperation at your patience and goodness, such a one secretly appreciates your efforts. And if this person can open the doors of his or her will (heart), you will be the first in line to enter.

Now, how would you go about attracting the will of a mature person — one whose will controls all actions?

The answer to that question depends very much on your own maturity as a person. The more solidly good you are, the more interest and desire you create in another. Solid, unpretentious goodness is contagious. It wants to share itself, and others want to share in it. This wanting to share is essential. If it is lacking, the goodness is shallow or counterfeit.

It is this creative, open goodness which mature persons have and which they seek in others. Memorized or mimicked goodness is like a silver- or gold-plated object. When the silver or gold of another's goodness wears away, the mature person is disappointed that what could have been is not.

It is not that way with "solid gold" goodness; it deepens with the years. When a man, for example, is presented with such a gift, he is beside himself. He rushes to meet the other. He wants to bring her home into his will, into his heart. To him, she is a glimpse of God. This is not supposed to happen until eternity, and yet it is happening right here and now — and to him.

This condition on the part of a man then overflows into the other. She, too, is beside herself. They are both beside themselves; they are ecstatic about each other.

How do you arrive at such solid goodness?

You work at it. You learn to rise above your senses, appetites, and feelings. You keep them under control. You learn to see and accept things as they are, until they can be realistically changed.

We will see more of this in the next chapter on the workings of your imagination and in a later chapter on true love of yourself.

Summary

We have seen in this chapter that there are a number of ways to attract others.

Physical beauty is only one kind of attraction. It is important and should be developed. Nature and art should work reasonably together out of consideration of yourself as a whole person. Many people who are not physically attractive find happiness nevertheless. Many people who are physically attractive — even exceptionally so — never find happiness at all. The happiness of each group depends on whether the other forms of attraction have been developed.

Before he was about to suffer and die, Christ said to his followers, "In my Father's house there are many dwelling places" (John 14:2). In a literal sense, he meant that there is room or a room for everyone in heaven. In a lesser sense, we can say the same about ourselves and others. There is a room, there are many rooms, inside of us for others to move into us and for us to move into them. Because one room is locked does not mean they are all locked.

Attraction has a kind of magic of its own. It can open the doors of your senses, appetites, feelings, as well as your mind and will. However, developing the potentials of your attraction is not magic. It takes awareness and work.

It is hoped these two chapters have made you aware of your potentials and how to develop them. It is also presumed that you are already working on them.

Many people in today's world cry out that they are not loved. They blame others for not loving them. But whether they will receive love depends so much on them. Each one of us determines — by the use of attraction — whether we will be loved at all.

Margaret

In her late thirties, Margaret is a very successful interior decorator. She is single.

Is Margaret single because she does not make herself attractive or because she does not find men attractive?

On the contrary. She appeals to men and men appeal to her. At the start of a new relationship her expectations would be high. But each time she came away disappointed. She would reach for something substantial in the other, yet never could find it. This made her so frustrated and angry that she wondered if there was something wrong with her. She thought to herself: "If I put such poor efforts into my work as men do into a relationship, I would be out of a job." Having sex seemed to be their only interest in life. To them, a good sex life spelled a good relationship.

Margaret was neither a prude nor a fool. So her protests about sex-dominated relationships were made as much from common sense as from conscience. She wanted a man with whom she could exchange deep feelings, a man she could talk to intelligently.

She did not think that was too much to ask from a relationship. She was willing to give as much. So should the other. If he could not, she would stay single until she found a person mature enough to let her deeper into his personality than the front rooms of his senses and appetites.

Bob

A married man in his early forties, Bob has three children. His wife's name is Tina.

Bob lost his parents in a car accident when he was seven. He and his two younger sisters were raised by their grandparents.

The death of Bob's parents left scars in his young life. He could not forgive them for leaving him and his sisters alone. Not being able to deal with his hurts, he hurried away from them as fast as he could. Unfortunately, running away from hurt became the pattern of his life. He could not, he would not, take life too seriously. He joked about everything.

This pattern worked for Bob, and that is how he attracted Tina. Tina had come from an unhappy background. Bob's way of making light of things helped her when she felt herself going under. They were good for each other.

Then Tina contracted a serious lung disease that threatened her life. She had to go away to a drier climate or die.

The next two years were exceptionally difficult for Bob and Tina. They both had to grow, to go deeper into themselves — more than either imagined was possible.

Bob found the scar paths of his old hurts, and he had to walk them and experience the pain he had hurried away from in his early life. Somehow it was not as bad as he felt it would be. Maybe it was because he had let Tina into deeper parts of him than he realized. She walked those paths with him.

At first, Tina feared the loneliness of separation from Bob and the children, but after a while she realized she was not alone. In one of her daily letters she wrote: "Bob, darling, the weight of my body holds me here, but my feelings, thoughts, and desires fly constantly to you and the children. I am not sure whether I am there or you are here. It does not matter. We are together. That matters."

Bob cried as he read those words, for he felt and thought the same.

He also felt forgiveness and love for his parents.

Questions

1. Other than physical appearance, what are the basic qualities that attract you to another? Do you seek someone with whom you feel at ease? What turns you off in your relationships with others?

2. Do you understand that when you are being loved you are the active person drawing another to you, and that when you are loving you are the passive person being drawn to another? How can this knowledge help you to improve your chances of being loved? What can you do to make yourself attractive or lovable?

3. Which of your senses most draws you to another? Is it sight — how another looks? Is it sound — how soothing and re-assuring another's voice is? Is it touch — how sensitively and magnetically another communicates by contact with you?

4. Are your appetites under your control or do they control you? What is your attitude toward sex? How important is it in your life?

5. Are you more attracted toward a ''feeling'' or a ''thinking'' person? Is your thinking free, or is it under the control of your senses, appetites, and feelings? Is your will free? Must it always seek what is pleasurable, or can it choose goodness when there is a conflict between what is pleasurable and what is good?

6. Do you feel that Margaret is a real person, or are her expectations too high?

7. Do you feel pity or admiration for Bob and Tina over the hard blows life has given them? Considering their personalities, do you think they would have learned the depth of love any other way?

Imagination:
Camera
of the
Mind

In our first two chapters we have examined the rhythmic movements of love and the various modes of attraction. Here we want to consider the important role of imagination in our love life. We hinted at this act or power of the mind on pages 32-34 in this book.

As a force, your imagination is like the hostess at a restaurant who brings you to your table.

As a place, your imagination is like a hallway leading to and from your senses, appetites, feelings, mind, and will.

A good part of your acceptance or rejection of another, therefore, depends on your imagination.

What is meant by your imagination, and what roles does it play in your love life?

Purpose of Imagination

Imagination is described as an act of the brain that takes or makes "images" of what your senses are reporting. It is like a camera. Its task is to give you an accurate image of the person or thing being reported. It is to this picture that your appetites, feelings, mind, and willpower will react.

This presents a problem.

Can your imagination give you an inaccurate picture of another? Worse yet, can it deliberately give you a false or fantasized picture of another? In either case, you obviously will not be relating to the other person as he or she actually is. What happens then?

Before attempting to answer these questions, it will help you get a clearer picture of your imagination if you realize that it is capable of two functions. Understanding these two functions, you will have some of the answers to the above questions.

Two
Functions

Your imagination can be informative and/or creative.

As a source of information, its task is to give you an accurate image of the person or thing being reported by your senses.

As a creative force, it can take these images and combine them with other images to form something entirely different. For example, it can join the wings of a bird to a horse, and make a winged horse or a galloping bird.

Both of these functions of your imagination can be very helpful.

The more your imagination is capable of sharp and detailed pictures, the more your appetites, feelings, mind, and will have to work on. Some persons can form such a detailed picture of what is happening around them. Others cannot.

Also, the more creative your imagination, the more ways other parts of you can relate to what is happening. Sex appeal, colorful feelings, a sharp mind, and a will convinced of the goodness of another — most of these come from a creative imagination. It enhances what is being reported. Poets, artists, and other highly skilled persons are all gifted with this creative talent. So, kept within the boundaries of basic realities and under the control of the whole person, such talent is precious.

But a creative imagination that ignores reality and refuses to be controlled by the whole person is like a kite without a string attached. There is no control over it. This is all right as long as it is flying high, but it can be a disaster when it comes crashing to the ground.

Both of these functions of your imagination can play a large part in your ability to love. And they should be free to do so. But they can be helpful or harmful in your pursuit of love.

Need for Supervision

Your imagination should be encouraged to function at its full capacity — both as a source of information and as a creative force. But there is also a need for supervision.

This need for supervising is necessary in several areas, three of which are fear, sexual passion, and "imagined" goodness.

Fear can drive your imagination, especially your creative imagination, to inconceivable lengths. It can make a mountain out of a molecule.

Sexual passion can cause you to have dreams about another that can consume you, at least for a time. When you awaken, you wonder whether you were hypnotized or drugged.

"Imagined" goodness can lead you to fateful mistakes. It is present when you are so taken by the "image" another presents that you feel you have finally found the attractive, intelligent, confident, and good person you have been seeking all your life. What insecurity is hiding behind that image is not immediately evident. Nor does your creative imagination care. It assumes and acts as if you have found the person who can fill the star role in your "they lived happily ever after" story.

Checking with Reality

So, while your imagination needs to be free to function well, it also needs watching. Of course, how closely you examine the reports of your imagination will depend on the subject matter. If you are dealing with matters of little or no importance, then it should be free to romp where it will. If you are dealing with matters of great importance, then it needs to be closely observed.

You need to learn how to check (harmonize) your imagination.

If you are entering a serious relationship with someone, go slowly. No realistic relationship happens all at once. A favorable introduction can happen suddenly and unexpectedly, but there are many steps to climb between an introduction and an established relationship. Creative imagination can eliminate those steps and elevate you to happy-ever-after heights, but when reality sets in and you fall down those steps that were eliminated, it will hurt.

Also, if you are establishing a relationship on the basis of potential, you need to be careful. There is often a great distance between the potential and the actual.

Does this mean that you should never take chances in starting a relationship?

No, it simply means being aware of the great difference between being "good looking" or "looking good" and being solidly good. It is easy for your imagination to be intrigued about how a person looks or how he or she could be, while overlooking how he or she actually is.

How can you tell the difference between imagined goodness and real goodness?

The difference will show up on its own. If you have the patience to give time to a relationship, and if you do not close your eyes when reality expresses a weakness in another, you will see what is real and what is only imagined.

Summary

Since your imagination is only the hallway of your being, it is not a good place for you or others to live.

The more reliable dwelling places, in their order of importance, are your appetites, feelings, mind, and will. It is when they take another into themselves that love appears on the scene. They depend on your imagination to give them an honest and colorful picture of another, but it is for them to check out the reports of your imagination. It can be very disheartening and lonely to find out later that the other person dwelling in these parts of you really is not the way he or she was imagined.

Tom

College-educated, good-looking, and single, Tom is the youngest of five children.

Tom's mother, Mary, constantly worries and prays for him because he is the only one in the family not "settled down." She expresses her concern to her husband, but he reassures her everything will turn out all right. "Just give him time," he says. Mary listens, but is not convinced. She knows her son. She knows his dreams and goals.

What are Tom's dreams and goals?

At an early age Tom began forming a picture of the girl he wanted to marry. In grammar school, he pictured her as pretty. In high school, he wanted her to be "popular." In college, he insisted that she be "sensitive and steady." Now, after many failures to find someone to match the picture in his mind's eye, he has decided to wait before looking again.

What is Tom really looking for?

He is looking for a woman who never existed but could have, if she had met the right man. As a child he listened to his mother's dream-talking. His imagination pictured the kind of person she secretly wanted to be. He wanted that picture for her and that kind of person for himself.

No wonder Mary understood her son so well. Would Tom

find what he was looking for, or would he compromise and settle for less? Somehow she felt he would not compromise.

Ann

At sixteen, Ann was unmarried, pregnant, and unhappy.

She had fallen madly in love with William, a senior in her high school. He was everything she imagined a boyfriend should be.

He was handsome.

He was strong.

He was intelligent.

He told her she was a special kind of person, the kind of person he had been looking for.

Ann treasured William. When she was not actually with him or talking to him on the phone, she dreamed of him constantly. Pictures of him filled her imagination. Despite the protests of her parents, he had moved into the inner rooms of her feelings and mind — and more. Ann felt there was no reason to wait until marriage to have sex. She felt she was married.

When Ann told William she was pregnant, he became very protective. He told her not to worry about anything. Graduation was only a month away. He would get a job and take care of everything.

That was three months ago.

Two months later William was away on a trip to Europe. It was his parents' graduation gift.

Today, William tells Ann he has decided to go to college, and suggests that Ann should have an abortion. If they got married or had a baby now, that would ruin everything.

Ann sat in the car, startled, as William made his plans for their future. Her hands were resting on the bulge of life within her. She started to cry.

"Don't do that," William said more harshly than he intended. "It's really the best thing for both of us. Can't you see that? Come down from the stars. Come down to earth."

Ann felt that she was not only falling from the stars, but they had all gone out. She felt William slipping away from her. She suspected he had been more a product of her imagination than a reality. It would take time, a lot of time, before her surfacing pain would heal her.

Questions

1. Are you an imaginative person? What does it mean to be an imaginative person? Does it mean you make up things that are not there, at least not there as you imagined them? Does it mean that you imagine or image things accurately? What is the difference between an informative and a creative imagination?

2. Do you have a creative imagination? Could you use a more creative imagination in relating to another? What are the good and bad points of a creative imagination? Do you tend to imagine the worst or the best in another?

3. How can you sharpen your imagination to give you a more detailed, accurate picture of what is happening? Can you slow down enough to give your senses a chance to react to what is happening and report it to your imagination? Or do your fears or wishful thinking speed up the reports of your senses, so that your imagination receives only a few details and cannot give you an accurate picture of what is happening?

4. Do you live and love mostly in the hallway of your imagination, or do you allow your real feelings, your mind and will, to play their parts? After years of living and loving are you easily

disappointed when things do not turn out the way you imagined they would and should? Do you feel and think there is something substantial in your life and relationships? What can you do to improve your life and relationships? Can you accept the discipline of reality and work from it?

5. What do you think of Tom? Are many of us influenced the way Tom was — with an imagined picture of another that was painted by our parents or some other childhood model? If this is the case, and the picture was formed when we had a young and creative imagination, is it a totally reliable picture to follow? Could we be chasing after an illusion and not realize it? Could this account for a great deal of disappointment in our relationships and why we do not put forth more effort to make them better?

6. What do you think Ann's experience with William is going to do to her? Will the reality of what is happening waken her from her favorite pastime — daydreaming? Or will it make her more of a daydreamer, since life has dealt her such a cruel blow? Would you spare Ann her pain if you could, or is her pain the string that keeps her in contact with reality? Do you sympathize with William, or does he need a shake-up to wake up?

4

Loving Another

Having considered the moving ways of love, attraction as a key to the doors of the heart, and imagination as the camera of the mind, we now look at the persons we are capable of loving and should love if we are to live a full life.

We will treat them in the following order. First, we will consider *other human beings* (in this chapter); next, we will consider *yourself* (in chapter five); finally, we will consider *God* (in chapter six).

As Christians, of course, we know that love of God is our top priority and that love of others is determined by our love of self.

You shall love the Lord your God
with your whole heart,
with your whole soul,
and with all your mind....
You shall love your neighbor as yourself
(Matthew 22:37,39).

But in the order of actual sequence we learn to love ourselves only after we have experienced love for and by others. And those loves make sense only after we come to realize that they must be based on our love of God. Our first awareness of love comes to us from our human family; later, it spreads to those outside that circle.

Why are you attracted to others? And what happens when you begin to love some special person? Your answer to these questions probably is, ''I don't know. I just feel that I love him or her and I want to be loved in return.''

Although that is an adequate answer, the underlying reason for love's attraction is that your being is like a deep well that needs to be filled by someone other than yourself. When you are attracted to another, you experience a flow from the parts of you that are attracted. If the flow is a fullness of favorable feelings and enriching goodness, you want the other near you — even within your being — to keep that love flowing. You never want to be cut off from the other. Even when the other person is not physically present, your thoughts and imagination reach out to him or her. You turn over in your mind and memory the deep impressions such a one has made on you. And as long as those feelings keep flowing, you feel full or at least partially full.

In this way, your love for another person can — as it were — prime the pump of your being. But in doing so there are two phases to be considered. Your love can show itself as a vital need or as a cherished want.

Love as a Vital Need

Right from the beginning of your life, God and nature provided you with all the equipment you would need to cope with life. It was all there — waiting to be used and developed.

In due time, these different parts of you — your senses, appetites, feelings, mind, and will — made you aware of the surrounding world. They also made you aware of yourself. They started within you a conscious flow that was pleasurable or painful depending very much on what was happening around you.

If the atmosphere was calm and loving, you absorbed that and felt calm and loved. There was nothing to keep you from experimenting with things and adding the input of such new experiences to your conscious flow. Should some of those experiences turn out to be painful, you could always run back to where it was calm and loving. Gradually, then, by recognizing and avoiding the experiences that produced pain, you began to acquire a confidence that you could handle life on your own.

If the atmosphere was disturbing and frightening, you absorbed that and felt disturbed and frightened. You tried in your own way to keep such painful feelings out of or away from your conscious flow. Probably, you made an effort to numb your senses to what was happening around you. You might still be waiting for someone to remove your fears and insecurities and replace them with calm and loving feelings.

In this latter case, you will need someone attentive, tender, and patient, someone special who will provide the love you had and lost — or never had at all.

This needful love can be found in what is called an ''in love'' relationship. It is the nature of such an experience for the two involved to be attentive, tender, and patient with one another.

They are so attentive that they want to be constantly with each other and to know everything that is happening. They want no look, touch, feeling, or thought to go unnoticed. They want to be a part of everything.

They are so tender that when one of them is hurting the other senses it immediately, and does everything possible to ease the pain. The gentleness of their demonstrations of love is refreshing.

They are so patient that even the mistakes that each of them makes are passed over or made light of. Their mutual faults acknowledged in this way actually bring them closer together.

There is a kind of magic to their love experience that is similar to that of a happy childhood. They run, play, and are as excited as children on a holiday. They even use baby terms of endearment.

Now, it is hoped that the person who enters such a relationship because of this needful love will be stimulated by this intense experience to reach out for more positive feelings. And, once started in this direction, he or she will sustain them and develop them.

But it should be noted that the intensity of a good "in love" experience lasts about the same length of time that a child needs to begin feeling special. With that feeling of worth as a foundation, the child — in this case the adult — is now prepared for the next step of growth.

What happens when a person is not ready to leave the intensity of an "in love" experience? He or she may seek out other "in love" experiences. Fortunately, however, most persons gladly accept the next step in their growth — "wanting" another instead of "needing" him or her.

Love as a Cherished Want

Persons arrive at wanting love either because they have learned to grow as a result of an "in love" experience or because the love they "needed" has already been provided by the calm and loving atmosphere in their own home.

In this experience you yourself fill the well of your being to share your fullness with someone else. This is especially true if the other is sharing his or her fullness with you. You automatically want to do the same. Somehow, by sharing yourself you become aware of treasures within you that probably would have been neglected except for this new relationship. The other's laughter or favorable comments over your wit, intelligence, and goals tend to make them more real to you.

So, although you do not *need* the other, you want him or her because of the mutual sharing of goodness between the two of you.

The difference between needing another and wanting another may be compared to the way people appreciate gold. Some love it for its material worth; others love it for its qualities of beauty and goodness. If you value gold for the goods it can buy, you are like the person who needs another for what he or she can give. If you value gold for its beauty and how its warm, shiny color lifts and fills your whole being, you are like the person who yearns for another for the purpose of sharing goodness with that person.

No human being is total goodness, but when the one loved has enough goodness to attract you and make you want to match that goodness, you have found a gold mine. The other is someone to be treasured. You yourself have wealth only now discovered.

This whole experience is so rich that it defies description. It leads to awe and gives a hint of how experiencing the solid goodness of God will be in the afterlife. (No wonder heaven is referred to as the beatific vision.)

Risks Involved

"This all sounds beautiful," you may be saying to yourself. "But what about the risks involved in going out to another? If this is such a rewarding experience, why do some people become recluses and turn to pets instead of persons for companionship? If they have built a wall around themselves, isn't it because they have been hurt or cheated in relating to others?"

Without a doubt you are taking chances when you undertake a relationship with another. But the extent of the danger depends on whether you go to another with a need for the other to fill your emptiness or with a desire to share your fullness.

If you go to another with a need, then much will depend on the maturity of the other person. If he or she is also in need, then the risks you are taking can be great. If you go to another with a desire to share from your fullness, the risks you are taking are much less. If the other also has a fullness to share, the risks are very small.

How can you gauge your own maturity and the maturity of the other?

This is not always easy to find out. Many persons — and you may be one of them — hide behind masks that make them seem secure. But once the mask is stripped away through an interchange of relating, you begin to realize what you are dealing with in yourself or in the other. That can be frightening; but it can also be an important learning experience.

Considering these risks, you might wonder if going out to another is worth it.

It is.

Even if you are insecure and do not find someone secure enough to help you, you will at least know how insecure you are, and can make plans to do something about it. Obviously, if you succeed in having a good or a workable relationship with another, the rewards are greater.

Summary

In this chapter we have examined what it means to love another person. We may be attracted to another because we *need* love — not having received it in the family circle. Or, having received love in the home, we may *want* love as a means of sharing our goodness with another. There are risks involved, but they are worth taking.

We will see in the next chapter that how well you love yourself will determine how well you relate to others.

Charles and Rose

After two dozen years of marriage and a grown child, Charles and Rose find themselves wondering where their love has taken them. They sense the same question in each other's eyes. "Who are we?" they seem to be asking each other. But the question remained unasked until Charles' drinking got out of hand. Forced to seek help, they both finally spoke the words, "Who are we?"

After two sessions together, the therapist told them he wanted to see them individually. When they asked why, he explained, "You are asking a double question when you use the word 'we.' You really need to ask yourselves individually, 'Who am I?' Some couples complement each other in their insecurities. One is a good talker, and the other is a good listener. One is good in a crisis but falls apart ultimately. The other is terrible in a crisis but can be very supportive when it is over. You do not complement each other. Actually, instead of cooperating, you are in competition. Your personal insecurities have almost bankrupted your marriage."

Charles and Rose sat stunned. They were looking for an easier solution. To work on themselves was not going to be easy. They told the therapist they needed more time to think about switching over to individual therapy.

In the meantime they looked around for another therapist who would treat them together. They found one, but several months later they questioned whether they had done the right thing. They could not answer that, but at least they had agreed on what they were doing. It was the first real cooperation they had shown in years.

Questions

1. What are your most vivid memories of having loved and been loved by another? Do they take you back to childhood? Are they the ''in love'' feelings of an actual or make-believe romance? Are they the memories of motherhood or fatherhood?

2. What parts of you dominate your conscious flow? Your senses bringing in their reports? Your appetites in search of fulfillment? Your feelings or lack of feelings? Your mind puzzling out your situation? Your will seeking or enjoying the good things of life? Your imagination creating things as you would want them to be? How do others stimulate these parts of your being?

3. Do you need others to calm your fears and give you a positive feeling toward life? If their positive flow stops, do you revert back to a negative flow?

4. Do you have an adequate positive flow of your own and want to share it with another? How does such sharing fill the well of your being?

5. Are you confused about your feelings of love? Do they sometimes seem to be coming from a need or from a child's level and at other times from a more mature level? Have you ever been ''in love''? What was it like? Did it seem that such feelings would never end? Did they end? If so, was there something solid about the relationship that kept it going? Are ''in love'' feelings only a fill-in for the lack of love in childhood? Can a mature person have ''in love'' feelings? What might be the difference between the ''in love'' feelings of an immature and a mature person?

6. Are you afraid of love — to love or be loved? Are you afraid of the risks? Have you been hurt or deeply disappointed in a relationship — when the other finally removed his or her mask?

7. What do you think of Charles and Rose? Do they sound familiar? Were they wise in rejecting the first therapist's suggestion of individual counseling? Was either ready for a confrontation with his or her self? Did they gain anything by choosing to do what they did?

5

Loving
Yourself

We saw in the last chapter that a person's first experience of love flows from family relationships. If this relationship is loving, you yourself develop a conscious flow of positive feelings; if the relationship is unloving, your feelings are negative.

This leads us to a consideration of good self-love. A true love of yourself is capable of supplying you with an abundance of positive feelings and more. It puts you in a position to have something worthwhile to share with another. The formula for loving others is based on true self-love. Jesus said, "You shall love your neighbor as yourself" (Matthew 22:39).

"But," you may object, "don't all persons instinctively love themselves? You don't have to make an effort to do that. What takes effort is when you go out to others."

Actually, it is not that simple.

We have just seen that if you received an overdose of rejection, put-downs, and shocking experiences from your surroundings, your constant conscious flow is more negative than positive. You do not approve of and love yourself. You find fault with yourself and begin to hate yourself. You tend to do the same to others. Whether the hatred shows or not, it is always there.

Obviously, if you have these negative feelings, you should not treat your neighbor as you treat yourself. Rather, you should treat another person as you *should* treat yourself — a person to be loved.

Meaning of
Self-Love

Basically, loving yourself means being united with and within yourself. This demands that your true "self" controls your entire life.

Your life is under control when you do not allow your appetites and feelings to dominate you. They can have more likes, wishes, wants, or "gimmes" than are good for them or for you as a whole person.

Your life is under control when you do not allow your imagination to get out of hand. This is especially true when it has painted an "image" of perfection you must follow. If you have been programmed to act in a certain way and you fail to perform properly, you suffer embarrassment, guilt, and self-hatred. You then begin to imagine that others are talking about you and thinking less of you. These circumstances may drive you to despair or to drink. But if you really love yourself, you will learn to control your imagination and make an honest judgment about yourself. Then you will begin to stand on your own two feet. Self-control is the basis of true self-love.

Immature Control

At this point you may be saying, "This sounds nice, but how do I arrive at such control over myself? My senses, appetites, feelings, mind, and willpower are supposed to be free to enter my flow of consciousness, aren't they? What is going to stop any one of them from overwhelming me and having its way? What can stop my appetite for sex from overpowering me with its strong physical and psychological demands? What can stop my feelings of fear from doing the same? What can stop the demands of my imagination — that I always present a perfect image — from paralyzing my consciousness with guilt? As these and other powerful forces invade my consciousness, what can I do to prevent them from taking over?"

These are questions that most persons find difficult, and even impossible, to answer. They have little or no control over such forces. At most they might try a system of opposing one force against another and hope that the one bringing the less pain will win out. Thus, they might oppose their need for a perfect image against the forces of their sexual feelings. Their fear of embarrassment or feelings of guilt may well win out over the forces of sexuality. Thus, if their image holds, and is not disturbed by alcohol or drugs, they have some fixed control over themselves.

Is such a method of control wrong?

No, it is not wrong. In fact, for the young and those who lack self-control, it is a fairly reliable method. Shame or embarrassment is such a powerful feeling that few are willing to run the risk of incurring it. That is why society — family, community, and religion — uses it.

Still, there are drawbacks to this approach. Shallowness and playing costly games with yourself are two of them. So, a better way of self-control should be found and used.

Mature Control

There is a better way of controlling your appetites and feelings than your "image" formed on the basis of what others expect of you.

This better way is the realization that you are, or are capable of being, a whole person. You are not your appetites or feelings. As filled with life as they are, they are not all of your life. They are only parts of it.

If you try, you can get your imagination to give you an "informative" picture of yourself as you are. It is a complete picture of you both exteriorly and interiorly. Now when you look at this picture of yourself as a whole person, it is obvious that you are more than any one part.

Using this picture of yourself as a whole person, you are in a position to listen to and control your individual parts. For example, when your appetite for food urges you to overeat, you — the whole you — can listen and delay your decision until you have consulted your feelings about the pain that your physical health will suffer, your mind about the truth that eating is for living and not vice versa, and your will about what is good for you as a whole person. Then you ask yourself the question: "Am I ready to accept the consequences of my action?"

This is not simply a question of risking the embarrassment that comes from destroying the image others want you to portray, nor does it come from the shame you would feel at upsetting them. Secretly, you may not care; or you may want to destroy the image they imposed. You may even want to upset them. No, the question in this case — and in other cases — is what do you, the whole you, choose to do?

Benefits of Mature Self-Love

Although it takes practice in picturing yourself as a whole person and using that image — not the one others have imposed — as a basis for judging your actions, the benefits are well worthwhile.

The *first* benefit is that it helps you make good judgments.

If you are accustomed to looking on yourself as a whole unit, no matter how vivid the reports and demands of your senses, appetites, and feelings, they cannot prevail over you the whole person. You will judge the value of each part. You will be fair, but you will also be wise. You will try to see what is best for your whole being — before, not after, you act.

If you are not accustomed to looking on yourself as a whole unit, you expose yourself to acting foolishly. You may hold a particular need so close that you cannot see whether it properly fits into your life or not. Others can see it, but you cannot.

A *second* benefit is that it brings you peace.

Peace is present when all is in order. Chaos or confusion are present when all is not in order.

Although it might seem more peaceful to give in to the clamoring demands of your individual parts, it is not. Only when you judge an action from the perspective of your whole personality do you insure yourself a maximum of good order and peace.

A *third* benefit is that it frees you to give the maximum of yourself to another.

As we have already seen, the act of loving consists of moving yourself into another's personality. A full, mature act of loving means moving all of you into the other. Would you not have to be in control of all of you to make such a full, mature act of love?

If your appetites or feelings control you, they would be moving in; but you would not be there as a whole person. And on tiring they would want to depart, leaving nothing, or almost nothing, of you in their place.

If only an image of what others want of you is in control, you are also heading for trouble. Hiding behind this image, you move into the other. What happens when the other tires of your shallowness and sees beyond the mask you are wearing? It could be disastrous for both of you.

Obviously, neither one of the above ways of entering another meet the requirements of true love. The first may satisfy for a time, and the second will prove inadequate once the masks are removed.

What a difference it is to enter another as a whole person. As yeast raises the dough of bread, so this mature approach lifts the relationship to a level that breathes with life.

This is true when you are loving and moving into or giving yourself to another. It is also true when you are being loved. Each lover wants to receive the other as a whole person, not just a part of one.

Beware of Counterfeits

In searching for a mature self-love you should learn to recognize the difference between immature and mature love.

It is easy to recognize a "gimme" self-love as immature. With some help you can also learn to recognize that the "image" others want you to portray is not the real you born of mature self-love.

But it is not so easy to recognize the immaturity of a self-love that has closed down your personality to protect you from hurt. This "closing down" consists of a severe control over the soft, tender, warm, affectionate, trusting side of your feelings.

If you have been hurt often by insensitivity and rejection, the trusting side of your feelings becomes enveloped with a protective covering. You begin to develop an "I don't care" attitude. You try not to care or get close to anyone. After some time a solid crust or a wall forms around the sensitive parts of your personality.

This attitude gives you control over yourself, but it is not a control coming from you as a whole person. No, it is a control based only on that part of you that resists past rejection by others.

The sad part of all of this is that it can happen when you are quite young, and you have learned to cover it over so well because your training insisted that you always act properly in the presence of others. Hardly aware of what is happening, you continue to function and appear to go out to people surfacely just as you have been told to do. It might take a long time before you fully realize that something is wrong.

It is clear that such an attitude is not the result of mature self-love. It may have been the only way to protect your sensitive feelings at the time. But it is hoped that you are in a position now to find a better way to protect them. You need those delicate feelings to make their contributions to your own personality and to a loving relationship with others.

Face Up to Your Fears

In your efforts to break the counterfeit control described above — or any other control born of immature self-love — your greatest enemy is fear. If you truly wish to become a united person, you will have to face fear head on.

While other parts of you tend to carry you away, fear can keep you hostage within yourself. It will not let you go until its demands are satisfied.

What can you do with a fear that practically paralyzes you?

Entire books have been written in answer to this question, and even these have not completely solved the problem. So be understanding if what is written here seems so inadequate for handling excessive fear.

The main point to remember is that a surface or conscious fear is usually not the real problem. The real fear is probably layers deep in your memory and nervous system. Surprisingly, the root fears feeding the surface fears might not be all that serious. They seemed overwhelming and impossible to solve at the time because of your overactive imagination and lack of help in coping with them. Now that you are older you should find it easier to cope with them.

A good way to face your fears is to step back slightly from them and ask yourself, "Who is going to win here? Am I going to win or are my fears going to win?" By drawing a line between yourself and your fears you begin your campaign to conquer them. If your fears cross over that line, you can call on your anger to help you. "I will not let a part of me get the best of me. I won't."

At first, these may sound like empty words; but slowly, perhaps with help, you will begin to make progress. As you face up to your surface fears, the hidden ones will reveal themselves. If you handle them in the same way, you will begin to control your fears. Listening to their warnings, you are able to see whether you want to act on them or not.

Summary

The importance of having a solid love for yourself should now be clear to you. If loving others, including God, seems to bring such poor results for you, maybe the fault is with you and how you treat yourself. Perhaps what you are doing or looking for is what makes love less than the treasure it should be.

Having discussed the real meaning of self-love, we have examined the difference between immature and mature self-love. And we have concluded that only the image of you as a whole person can give you a mature self-love.

We have all heard the expression, "Love or charity begins at home." In the area of self-love this means putting the house of your own personality in order so that both you and others can be at home there. Then you are in a position to love others as you love yourself.

Ernie

Ernie is a fifty-five-year-old lawyer who has never married. He looks much younger than his age, but his personality growth has not kept pace with his physical maturity.

Ernie has never been comfortable with himself. He can function as a lawyer because his head is a file cabinet of rules — the dos and don'ts he learned as a child and those he learned in law school. He must give every rule its strictest interpretation. He is too frightened to act differently.

It is obvious that Ernie does not love himself.

First, he is not even aware that he has a self. He is only aware of a set of rules which take the place of self.

Second, these rules — not love — direct him; they are like a fence completely surrounding him. They determine everything. Rarely do they give him any peace.

One day while Ernie was browsing in a bookstore he spied a book that set him thinking. The book was entitled *How to Develop a Better Self-Image.**

"That is what I need," he told himself. As he read he became more and more convinced of his need to change. He read the book eagerly and looked for more like it. He was surprised and pleased to find himself and his condition portrayed in so many books.

Ernie has opened the doors of self-discovery. He has also opened the doors of love.

*I wrote this book for Liguori Publications. It explains in further detail how a person often confuses the "image" formed by others with his or her real self.

Questions

1. What were your previous ideas about the meaning of "loving yourself"? Was it a good, bad, or selfish thing to do? Have your ideas changed as you read this chapter? What does it mean to be united with yourself?

2. Some persons form the "image" of themselves by basing it on what others expect of them. Is this wrong?

3. Can you reach and retain an image of yourself as a whole person? How can that help you to avoid overeating and going to excess in regards to sex? How can it keep the parts of you under your control? How does seeing yourself as a whole person affect the gift of yourself that you give to another?

4. Are you familiar with the counterfeit self or counterfeit control of yourself that comes from "not caring"?

5. What problems do you have in dealing with your fears? Do they tend to go overboard and take you with them? Is there anything you can do about them?

6. Does this chapter help you better appreciate loving yourself? Are you at home within yourself or do you constantly distract yourself from your inner feelings about self?

7. Do you love yourself?

8. Has Ernie loved himself? Do you feel he can change enough to discover and love himself?

6

Loving God

No one has ever seen God.
Yet if we love one another
God dwells in us,
    and his love is brought to perfection in us
(1 John 4:12).

Although God is the source and foundation of our love for others and for self, we do not actually come to a knowledge of his love until we have experienced the kind of human love we have described in the last two chapters. It is hoped that what we have learned about human love will give us a better understanding of God's love.

Getting to Know God

Your first knowledge of God probably came from your parents. When you were a child they told you about the objects you were beginning to see and touch, and they gave them names. They told you about the people in your life, and they gave them names. "I'm Mommy. Say 'Mommy.' " "This is Daddy. Say 'Daddy.' " And they explained to you about God. "That is God. Say 'God.' "

During those early years you gradually came to know more about God. Later, your knowledge and acceptance of God was probably reinforced by religion teachers.

How long can such an approach to God last?

It can last a long time, even a lifetime. Or it may last only a short time. For example: If you were to lose respect for your parents and religion teachers or if you were to meet with too much guilt or too many letdowns, any of these could cut you adrift from God.

What happens then?

Some do without God. They place him in the class of other make-believe characters whom they say they have outgrown — for example, Santa Claus or the bogeyman.

Others are never sure. They do not deny God, but neither do they affirm him. They drift along in a neutral position.

Most of us, however, open our eyes, feelings, and mind to examine the world in which we live. From the wonders that surround us, we realize that someone special must have fashioned the fascinating flowers, the open fields, and the smiling faces of loved ones. They realize that many of these wonders are open to improvement. They need further attention and endeavor on our part to complete them. This can bring up many questions about suffering and evil, but it also brings out the remarkable intelligence of the person who designed these wonders. He has left room for human beings to use and develop their intelligence and willpower to help perfect creation. He is like a father who leaves a partially finished project in his workshop for his son to puzzle out and complete. They both get satisfaction when the task is brought to a successful conclusion. It is in this way that we confirm the knowledge of God that others have taught us.

There is also another method of finding God or getting to know him. He has revealed himself in Sacred Scripture, the Holy Bible, which is composed of the Old and New Testaments.

In the Old Testament, when we set aside the scenery, the people, and the dramatics of some of the stories, we see that God is making known some rather simple truths about himself. They needed to be said to clear up some misleading beliefs about God.

Consider the account of Noah and his ark. The message of the story is that God does not act on mere whim and destroy people because he is mean, bored, or just feels like it. People seemed to believe that God — like the creatures he created — could and would act irresponsibly. The story says that this is not true. It does not deny physical disasters, but it insists that these disasters only destroy us if we have lost our moral integrity and strength. So, instead of being frightened because we do not know what an irresponsible God may inflict on us, we should seek to be at peace because God is not that way. If God allows us to be challenged, he also gives the needed support to face the challenge and profit by it.

In the New Testament God acts out such a tremendous love story that we will reserve a whole chapter to tell it. It will serve as a fitting conclusion to this book on love.

In their own ways, both Testaments try to give us a peek at God and how he acts toward us.

God's Loving Approach

Since the process of love is a kind of "moving in," it is easier to understand and picture God being in you than you being in God. We will therefore consider being loved by and receiving God first.

That God loves you is a solid truth of reason and revelation. Good reasoning concludes that it is God's love that has brought you into being. If he stopped loving you, you would stop being. Revelation proclaims this in a beautiful passage:

Can a mother forget her infant,
  be without tenderness for the child of her womb?
Even should she forget,
  I will never forget you
(Isaiah 49:15).

If you accept the fact that God loves you and you want to leave your doors open to him, what are the ways he can enter?

An important but the least stable way is through your senses and feelings. When you sense and feel God's presence because of something you have seen, heard, or experienced, you are overwhelmed. Like a sweet-smelling incense, a sensation of well-being and joy fills your whole being. And with Peter on the hilltop, you exclaim, ''Rabbi, how good it is for us to be here!'' (Mark 9:5)

A less intense but more stable way for God to enter is by way of your mind and will.

Your mind seeks after truth. Your will seeks after what is good. Once you realize that the truth and goodness of things and people are coming from the power of God, you can reach beyond them to God himself. Your mind and will take delight in focusing their attention on him. In doing this they have let God into deep places within you. Like a sponge in the depth of the ocean that contains water and is surrounded by water, you contain God and are surrounded by him. That is why Christ could say:

Anyone who loves me
will be true to my word,
and my father will love him;
we will come to him
and make our dwelling place with him
(John 14:23).

And Saint Paul would add, ''You must know that your body is a temple of the Holy Spirit, who is within — the Spirit you have received from God'' (1 Corinthians 6:19).

Now this awareness of the presence of God by means of the senses, feelings, mind, and will is immediately available to everyone. But there is another way to God — through holy or sacred signs.

God and religion use certain signs or symbols to help you

74

make contact with God. They are very helpful because you can see and touch them and know that God is present and is using them to communicate with you. They are visible-invisible contact-makers with God, that is, external activities that put you in touch with an unseen God.

The most important of these contact-makers are called sacraments. A sacrament can be described as follows:

It is a simple human action that God uses to express a higher reality. A human minister does an action on one level, and God raises that action to a higher level.

Consider Baptism, for example. Using water and specific words, a minister washes the person presented for the ceremony. What is God doing? He is doing the same thing. He is washing the person free of sin or guilt. He is accepting him or her into a special relationship with himself. God is saying, "You are not only my creation, you are my son, my daughter. I have given you a new life. I have given you a special sharing in my own life. Enter into a close relationship with my other sons and daughters."

So the sacraments are special doors to and from God. You step through a sacrament to God himself, and God moves into you to accomplish a task and give you a special contact with him.

Your Loving Response

That God can enter you in so many ways is a reality that surpasses all other realities. Imagine, you have God in you.

But how do you respond to God's loving approach?

Since God is a spirit he does not have senses, appetites, or feelings. He has a mind and a will; he *is* mind and will. In loving God, then, you are attempting to enter his mind and will.

How can you do that?

In one way, you are already in God's mind and will. They sustain you in being.

In another way, by your act of love you want God to do more than sustain you. You want him to think of you and take you into his will with delight. You want to be his friend.

If you feel and think through your being in God in this special way of love, you will find it as marvelous a reality as having God in you. It will motivate you to achieve your maximum goodness. You want to bring with you as much goodness as you can.

A make-believe goodness will not do.

A fanatical goodness will not do.

Only a goodness that is real will do.

You are in the mind and will of God. It is not possible for you to find a better place to be.

"But," you may object, "I am one of those who is never sure of God. I am numb about him. There are times when I would like to believe in God and be comforted by my belief. There are other times when I feel that belief in God would suffocate my intelligence and spoil my life-style. I am confused."

Your confusion might not be a bad sign. It is painful, but it is not necessarily bad. You are like a traveler who arrives at a fork in the road. Both roads are unmarked. "What should I do?" the traveler says. "Should I wait here for someone to give me directions, or should I take a chance and drive on, unsure?"

If you have been waiting for someone to show you the reality of God, perhaps this book will reveal the way. What has been written here makes sense. It is in contact with reality. It is not dealing with fantasy. Fantasy is all right in its proper place. You do not need fantasy when you are dealing with God. God is reality. Reality has its foundations in God. Take away God and you take away the foundations of reality. All then becomes a dream. There is no cause and effect. All is make-believe. And love is an illusion.

But love is not an illusion, and God is definitely a reality. If you do not acknowledge this and open the doors of your heart to him, your heart will be lacking the one person who can really fill it.

This real God is therefore important for your life and your love.

He is as important to your life as deep roots are to a tree or running water is to a riverbed. Without deep roots, the tree cannot flourish. Without running water, the riverbed becomes a swamp. Your life, without the deep roots of God or an open contact with the refreshing flow of his being, is like a weed in a garden. A weed may look good and may grow sturdy and tall, but it is only a weed.

God is as important to your love as a third leg is to a three-legged table. If your love is only for others and for yourself, something is lacking. There is no proper balance. You can try desperately to fill your heart with loving others or with self-love, but there are deep spaces within you that remain unfilled. You can attempt to cover over those spaces with human love, as one might cover over a well with wooden planks; but one day those loves will not hold. When you least expect it, you will fall through to the deep spaces below and will wonder what is wrong. You thought you had everything you would ever need, but now you feel so empty.

These are mostly negative reasons why God is so important to your life and love, but there is an even more powerful and positive reason. It is this: God is important because God is God

This reminds us that God is responsible for everything. As the design artist, he has fashioned us and placed us on the canvas of creation. And if our lives are to be the masterpieces that he envisioned, there are certain areas where only he wields the brush.

Talking to God

Once you understand this personal love between God and you — that he is within you and you are within him — it is perfectly natural to talk with God.

That presents a problem. How do you talk with someone whose voice is not audible? A one-way conversation does not sound very interesting. It is like talking to yourself. Surely there has to be a better way.

There is.

One of the best ways to converse with God is by silent gazing. Have you ever shared your presence with another and had another share his or her presence with you by simply looking or gazing at each other? The experience requires no words. You are a word. The other is a word. Together, you are two words, "I" and "you." Love has its own word, "am." Love, then, unites you two and completes the sentence, "I am you."

Beautifully, the word that is each of you is so full of meaning that it could take you hours, days, even years to arrive at complete understanding.

What a filling, fulfilling, experience this is. It will be one of your favorite joys in eternity.

Is this the only way to carry on a conversation with God? Of course not. Any way that is comfortable for you will do.

Listening to God

Although we have said that we cannot actually hear God speaking to us, he does communicate with us through Revelation — as we have seen — and he likewise speaks to us through our consciences. And this is the reason why some persons never find him or, having found him, desert him. Because they have not listened to God through the voice of conscience they raise a wall between themselves and him. The name of that wall is guilt. It causes them to avoid anything that could remind them of God. Guilt and God are incompatible.

Sometimes, however, the actions that produce guilt are the result of an immature attempt to satisfy a childish need or desire. If the person had been more mature, he or she would have avoided seeking such childish pleasures or ways of ventilating frustrations over an unfair situation.

Obviously, this does not take away the guilt or eliminate the responsibility to find more acceptable ways of getting satisfaction or ventilating feelings. But it does point out the fact that those who turn away from God because of such conduct should examine their growth factor with an eye for improvement. They need to grow. Once they do that, they will have very little difficulty in finding God and having a meaningful relationship with him.

By listening to God in this way they will begin to develop a mature love of self.

Summary

Here we have seen that our knowledge of God comes to us from our parents and from God's own revelation about himself in

Sacred Scripture. We have also examined what it means to be loved by God and how his presence in our lives affects us.

Next, we considered our response to his love and what this demands of us. It means talking to God as one who loves us and listening to him as one who wants to guide us. By doing these two things we learn to love ourselves and others in a more mature manner.

Dorothy

In her forties, Dorothy is a widowed mother of six growing children. Her husband, Donald, was killed five years ago. His death was the start of a powerful search for answers that led to a deeper Dorothy and a deeper relationship with God.

Dorothy was a practical person. Imagination was only for poets, she thought. A fork was a fork, and its only purpose was to be used as a fork. It was not an imaginary tree standing in a hill of mashed potatoes, as Donald would show the children. It was a fork.

After Donald's shocking death and the tearful wake and funeral which followed, Dorothy insisted on getting things back to normal in the family.

This routine worked for a while, but for the first time in her life Dorothy started having severe headaches. She went to her family doctor who could find nothing physically wrong with her. Tactfully, he asked her if she knew someone with whom she could talk. She said she knew a clergyman who might be helpful.

As she went for her weekly sessions it became clear to her counselor that Dorothy's practical approach to life was to avoid the pain of disappointment. As a child she believed everything, especially promises. "But you promised," she would cry when a grown-up failed to live up to expectations. Because she was disappointed so often, she convinced herself not to believe in anyone or anything until it was fact.

Dorothy took this approach with God. She would accept only what she saw. She would not believe in something she could not see. Donald was gone. She could see that. Her mind balked at where he might have gone.

Dorothy's counselor listened sympathetically to her hurt and anger. He did not try to stop her crying or feeling sorry for herself. He knew that by emptying herself of her resentments she would leave her childishness and learn to see beyond the here-and-now reports of her senses, appetites, and shallow, impulsive feelings. She would learn when to trust and when not to trust. He knew that once she learned to deepen herself, she would want to fill that depth with hope, with love, and ultimately with God.

After extended efforts, this is what happened. Dorothy took on more mature attitudes and began to grow in her appreciation and relationship with others and, especially, with God. He is now her best friend.

Questions

1. How have you come to know God? Do you know him through the experiences and reasoning of others? Or have you conducted your own search for him and succeeded in finding him on your own? Do you rely more on the testimony of the Scriptures or on your own reasoning? Do the two help each other?

2. How can God move into you? What is a sacrament and how does it work?

3. How do you move into God? Do you find it exciting to

realize that you can be in the mind and will of God in a loving, comforting way?

4. What do you do when you have difficulties in finding or understanding God? Do you let the clouds overwhelm you and hide him from you, or do you pull to the side of the road and wait — for your own clarity to come, for you to grow, for God to show you a way that you can use to return to him?

5. How important is God to your life, to your love?

6. Are you familiar and comfortable with the silent language of gazing? Does it sound strange to carry on a conversation without words or only with the word of your being?

7. What do you think of Dorothy? Are you like her? Do you accept only what you can see, hear, or touch? What is lacking in such an approach to love, to God?

7

Love's Unifying Power

Having examined what it means to love another, yourself, and God, we are now in a better position to consider the marvelous unifying power of love. Without destroying their individuality, love can make two different people think and act alike. In the last chapter we mentioned that the verb *love* is equivalent to the verb *am*. "I love you" then becomes "I am you."

We treat this unifying power of love here in order to avoid possible confusion and to point out the dangers that come from a misunderstanding of this power of love. As a normal human being you prefer to relate to someone who has something in common with you rather than to someone totally different.

So, in the first stage of love you seek someone who sees, feels, and thinks the way you do. On finding such a person, you begin your journey toward oneness.

In the second stage both of you tend to become more and more like each other. Gradually, you work on the rough parts of your personalities until they become smooth, allowing both of you to mesh as if there were no spaces in between. These rough parts are the same ones that tended to destroy your own personal identity before you gained a mature love of yourself. Somehow, in loving and being loved by another you possess more of yourself, and in loving yourself more you are in a position to love another more.

As you can see, this oneness can be, or wants to be, a total experience. It will start with less and work toward more. And, as an experience, it will relate to both God and yourself.

Oneness with God

Wanting to be like God — to be one with him — is as old as the human race. But it can be a false, pride-filled desire or a true, loving desire.

The story of the temptation in Eden (see Genesis 3) is an example of prideful desire to be like God. And that same story is repeated in today's world by all those who desire and strive to be what they are not.

But a true, loving desire to be one with God is entirely different. Love demands equality between those who love. Between human beings, "I love you" means "I am you, your equal." You can never claim full equality with God, but Christ gave you a kind of equality when he said to his apostles:

I no longer speak of you as slaves,

for a slave does not know what his master is about.

Instead, I call you friends,

since I have made known to you all that I

heard from my Father"

(John 15:15).

By sharing this intimate knowledge with you Christ makes you one with him. This, then, is one form of oneness with God.

Another form of oneness with God comes from the fact that you are a person. God is a person. You are a person. As the "image" of God (see Genesis 1:27), you are capable of thinking and willing. You are also free to acknowledge or not acknowledge God, to love or not love God. What a tremendous amount of godly power that is.

A third and most meaningful way of becoming one with God is provided by the gift of supernatural life. Because God loves you — wants to become one with you — he gives you a sharing in his intimate life. It will take you the whole of eternity to fully understand and appreciate this.

In speaking of the natural life Christ said:

There is no greater love than this:

to lay down one's life for one's friends

(John 15:13).

We, too, can say the same about God's gift of the supernatural life: "There is no greater love than this: to *give* one's life for one's friends."

Oneness with Yourself

This oneness also relates to your love of self. When you love yourself in a mature manner, your senses, appetites, feelings, mind, and will work together as a unit. Each part is meant to serve you the person. If one part rebels against you, the person, you do not have a mature love of yourself.

When all your parts serve you in this way you possess a deeper awareness of yourself as a person. No one part of you exerts more pressure than it should. Through one part you can communicate all of you to another and can receive all of another in the same way. Your "I" is the "memory bank" where all the reports from your parts are stored. You — your person — remain one, even when your actions or functions differ. All this is true of a mature self. But if your "I" is not a mature self, then it will be a shadow and follow the lead of your senses, appetites, or feelings.

It is this oneness within yourself that gives you your identity: that something within you that remains one and the same. When that something is your mature "I," then you have a proper identity. You have a oneness — a solidarity, a wholeness — amidst a great number of changes and differences.

Dangers to be avoided

There are certain dangers attached to this amazing power which makes you one with the person you love. You may reach a false or mistaken oneness, and you may achieve a oneness that interferes with the individual growth of one or the other.

This first danger — reaching a mistaken oneness — can be avoided if you refrain from becoming a mere shadow of the other. It is easy to copy or follow another's lead, but the resulting oneness is only a veneer. It might be a workable combination between an aggressive and a passive person, but it is too shallow for a mature love.

The second danger — interfering with the growth of the other — can be avoided by reminding yourself that love seeks expansion, not restriction. Your oneness with another should encourage each of you to grow to a maximum capacity. The more each has, the more there is to share. Of course, this can only happen if there is cooperation, not competition, between the two pooling their resources of personality.

So, "I love you" does not mean "I annihilate you." It does not mean that you must always feel, think, or be drawn to the same things that appeal to the other. No, it means that whatever *you* have is mine and whatever *I* have is yours. It does not enrich either person if both have the same things. Rather, it stimulates both persons to become themselves and thus share their mutual treasures in a joint account.

At this point you may object. "But, doesn't this independence produce a self-centeredness that takes away from togetherness?" Isn't "I" a stronger trump card than "we," so that "I" wins over "us"?

It could, but then the love is not mature. Such persons are governed by "image" or motivated by "gimme" emotions. To allow and encourage such individuals to grow would be harmful to the relationship. Neither of those personalities should be allowed total freedom.

But, if the personalities involved are motivated by mature self-love as described in chapter five, then to allow each one freedom to become or work out the fullness of his or her personality is beneficial. It is even a necessity. Why? First of all, real self-love requires it. Second, only such a real self can make a total, giving exchange. If, in your efforts to achieve oneness, you prevent your real personality or another's real personality from growing, you are not acting maturely. Your action is not real love. It is the death of a personality. Eventually, it brings on the death of a relationship.

Again, you may object, ''I don't completely understand. What are all these personalities I am capable of being? Do you mean I can be a different person at different times?''

Yes.

Observe yourself closely. When you are ''showing off'' or when you become embarrassed over something you have done wrong, your ''pompous I'' is in control. When you do something that enhances your self-image, your ''pompous I'' rushes in to show the good you have done. Of course, it hides when you do something wrong. It is this ''pompous I'' that needs to be always right. It needs constant praise from others. It gets violent or moody when it is opposed or neglected.

You also recognize when your ''childish I'' is in control. It pouts when it does not get what it wants when it wants it.

Once again the importance of a good understanding of yourself and the development of mature self-love is evident. It is one of the most important keys to the doors of love.

And because it is so important, perhaps it would be good to review chapter five and, then, reread this chapter.

Recognizing and accepting differences

Now, let us suppose you have succeeded in avoiding the dangers described above. What happens if one person outgrows the other? Let's say that you both began in the ''childish'' stage or in the ''image'' stage, but you yourself have now become mature. Should you wait and encourage your partner to grow? What if he or she will not make a sufficient effort to do so?

This presents a serious problem that can have several answers.

One answer is that the more mature person can accept the immaturity of the other and try to make the best of it.

A second answer is that the more mature person can be patient while encouraging the other to change and motivating him or her to make the necessary changes.

A third answer is that the more mature person can decide that the imbalance is so great that he or she severs the relationship.

All of this unequal relating can be extremely painful for both, especially if it happens in marriage. Once the glow of the ''in love'' attraction or the flow of distracting activities wears off, the two may find themselves alone with themselves and confronted with such a problem. What will they do? Ideally, they should face it and work on it as soon as they detect the differences of maturity; otherwise, valuable time and good will could be wasted. Once disappointment settles into indifference or bitterness, the chances for saving the relationship become very small.

It should also be noted here that you may be faced with a somewhat similar problem with regard to your love of God.

Despite your oneness with God as indicated on page 85, you are vastly different from God and he is vastly different from you. How can you cope with such differences and keep your love relationship alive?

You can cope with such differences if you learn to think and will like God.

How does God think and will?

God's actions are total actions. Because he is not limited he does not think or will in parts or steps. He knows and wills his whole action here and now. Before his action becomes manifest to us, it is already in progress. When light comes to the earth from a star, you do not see it until it is already on its way. In the same way, God's action is complete, but it will take stages of time before you realize or see the fullness of his action.

In practical terms, what does this mean?

It means that you learn to trust and accept God — his way of knowing and willing — even though you do not see the total action and how it has your good as its goal. It means that you accept the painful parts of reality with a confidence that God is on your side and wants to help you profit by the situation.

In a way, however, you can also approximate God's whole-action approach, and you do this when you act as a whole person. Having looked over the situation and having received the reports of all your parts, you have your complete action in your head. You might not execute it immediately, but it is already in progress.

This is on your part. On God's part, he waits for your trust and acceptance. He encourages you to act as a whole person. That is why he made you in his own image and likeness.

Coping with your own immaturity

Once you have dealt with the differences you find in others and in God, your next step is to examine your own various stages of growth. How will you cope with the immaturity you find there?

Although your "real I" — not the "image I" of your training or the "childish I" of your immature feelings — is now stable and one, it has so much room for expansion it can frighten you.

Life growth can be compared to balloon inflation. It takes a strong effort to get the balloon to expand. You can feel your ears bursting as you blow air into it. In a similar way, each initial effort toward new growth takes a strong effort. You find yourself resisting what is happening. Your training and feelings will rebel; they are frightened of the outcome. And as you try to deal with them, you begin to have your own doubts about what is happening. You are like Columbus sailing the unknown seas. The maps you have to work with are not that good. You are afraid of what awaits you.

All of this is normal.

Most of it is necessary.

You do not know how to cope with what is happening. How could you? Facing the unknown is one of the major phases of growth toward maturity. If you already know or have previously experienced what is happening, you would not be going on to new growth. Actually, these growth changes are like little deaths making way for more life.

"But should the process be so frightening?" you ask. "Are there any reassurances along the way?"

There are.

First, you would not be where you are if you had not already grown considerably.

Second, this is where your acceptance and trust in God's caring can help immensely.

Third, you can seek the help of others who have experienced similar problems in their lives.

Seeking your identity

Some people who are set in their ways have nothing but scorn for persons who take time off to find themselves. This sounds so strange to them. "Imagine, grown men and women trying to find themselves. What nonsense!"

Obviously, such an endeavor can be nonsense. It can be a justification for acting in a childish, irresponsible way. This is especially true if it is done without giving it some serious thought or talking it over with someone capable of providing guidance. It can be used as an escape from loneliness or through fear of entering the unknown alone. It can be based on a fear of losing control over the other person and his or her development.

But it can and should be a very profitable experience. Great men and women have found this necessary, from time to time, to slow down the course of their lives and to take a good look at the quality of their living. They need time and space for themselves.

So, in love, although there is a driving desire for oneness, there is also a need for individuals to develop themselves according to their potential. This should not take away from their oneness with the loved one. Actually, it gives each of them more to share. Working out everything together and not leaving provision for the individual to develop aspects of his or her personality privately can be crippling.

Love, then, does not weaken when one seeks to strengthen himself or herself with the purpose of bringing that strength into the relationship.

Summary

This chapter has presented the unifying power of love. By becoming one with God and one with yourself you place yourself in a position to love another more. After examining the dangers to be avoided in seeking this unity, we reviewed the importance of recognizing and accepting our differences, coping with our own immaturity, and seeking our own identity.

We concluded by emphasizing that the stronger our own love is, the stronger will be our love relationship with another.

Frances

One day, as she looked back over her fifty years of living, Frances realized that her entire life was but a repetition of the patterns she established while quite young.

As an only child, she was curious about everything. She pestered her mother with endless questions. The only way her mother could get some relief was to tell her to wait until her father came home. She would. No sooner did he appear in the house than she would start popping her questions. He would pretend annoyance, but the gleam in his eyes showed the annoyance was not real or at least not deep. Her parents did not have to ask Frances questions during supper. Frances asked them.

When Frances went to parochial school she took her question-box personality with her. Secure teachers welcomed her questions. Insecure ones found them a threat. "Why can't you be like the other students? Why do you have to be different?" they would ask her. But welcomed or not, Frances asked her questions. "If I have to be quiet in church because it is God's house," she would ask, "is it because God is always sleeping and everything has to be quiet? Doesn't God like people to ask him questions?"

As the years rolled on, Frances grew into a beautiful woman. Men found her very attractive. She would ask them, "What do you want out of life?"

Some would answer, "You."

"What about me attracts you?"

"Your beauty," they would say.

"If I were not beautiful, you would not want me? I see."

Then she would walk away, leaving her admirers questioning what they had said or done wrong.

As Frances looks back over her fifty years — her marriage, her children, and her life — she appreciates the deep bond of love she has with all of them. She marvels how she can be so much like her husband and children, and yet, different. Love did not take her questioning mind away from her. Her husband, like her dad, pretends to be annoyed over the questions, but the gleam in his eyes shows that the annoyance is not real or at least not deep. He knew from the beginning there would never be a dull moment with Frances. There would be quiet, deep moments, but not dull ones.

Questions

1. Why do you want someone you love to feel, think, and will the same as you feel, think, and will?

2. How can you be one with God? How can you have a oneness within yourself?

3. What are the dangers involved in trying to be one with another, even if it is God?

4. Do you recognize when your "image I," based on your training, is in control of you and trying to control others? Do you recognize when your "childish I" is in control? How can their self-seeking destroy a relationship? Why don't the attempts of your "real I" to grow and be independent destroy a relationship? Is it better in a relationship to be totally dependent, completely independent, or interdependent (where both partners pool or share their independence)?

5. Have you been in a relationship where there has been a difference in growth? How did you cope?

6. What do you think of Frances? Would you like her as a friend? Would her questioning bother you?

Love's
Enemies

The preceding chapters of this book have concentrated on the positive aspects of love. Here we will consider the opponents of love. We list them in general as enemies; but, as we shall see, the underlying purpose of the emotions treated here is to protect us from pain and evil. It is only when they are allowed to go uncontrolled that they become enemies. The ones we will treat specifically are hate, fear, anger, jealousy, and sadness.

Hate

The most obvious enemy of love is hate, which — in its opposition to pain and evil — often produces loneliness.

As love is a uniting force, hate is a separating force. It can alienate one person from another. It can separate you from yourself, your real self.

If hate is in your senses and feelings, it is their reaction to pain inflicted by something or someone. It could be a physical pain — a bruise, a cut, a wound of some kind. It could be a psychological pain — an embarrassment or a rejection. But no matter what kind of pain it is, your senses and feelings want nothing to do with it. They push away from or hate the person who inflicted it or did not prevent it. And to make sure that it will not happen again, they post guards on themselves to avoid the circumstances that occasioned it.

When the hate stops in your senses and feelings, it is simply a body reaction to pain. When it reaches your mind and will, it has invaded your spiritual side. You reject that thing or person as a poison that can destroy you. You see them as evil.

And what is evil? It is the absence of a good that should be present. It is a physical evil, for example, when a person suffers the loss of an arm or leg. It is a moral evil when a person lacks what he or she should have for the fulfillment of his or her personality — the lack being caused by deliberately refusing to pursue a good or willfully turning away from it. An example would be a married man cheating on his wife. He could and should practice discipline and fidelity, but he chooses to let his sexual appetite take over and scar his relationship and personality.

So, evil differs from pain. Evil is something or someone that causes a loss of goodness. Pain is a reaction to something or someone that causes displeasure.

But it should be remembered that it is dangerous to take things or persons at face value. What looks good may not be good for you as a whole person. And what looks bad may actually be good for you as a whole person.

The difference, therefore, between pain and evil is this: Pain is present when the thing or person is not pleasing to your senses and feelings. Evil is present when the thing or person is unpleasing and therefore unacceptable to your mind and will — to you as a whole person.

Knowing this, it would seem only natural to hate all pain and evil. But it should be noted that nothing in this world is totally free of these two culprits. Even the things or people that give you pleasure or fulfill you as a whole person have limitations. It is painful when another runs out of the pleasures he or she has been giving you. It is an evil when another's exchange of goodness falls short because of his or her lack of maturity.

What do you do when you experience these limitations? Do you close your eyes and your heart to avoid the pain or evil? You could do that, but how long will you be able to stand it? Besides, what kind of living and sharing is it to go through life with your eyes closed or only partially open?

One way to solve this problem is to recognize that it is possible to love and hate a person at one and the same time. You can love the pleasure and goodness the other shares with you and hate the pain and evil that happens to accompany it. Somewhere along the way you may have to strike a balance between the pleasure and goodness or the pain and evil. If the other person has attained a measure of solid maturity, the pleasure and goodness will outweigh the pain and evil. And if there is evident striving for maturity, it will eventually happen. Obviously, it would be foolish to close the doors of your heart to someone on the threshold of self-discovery and maturity.

Hate causes loneliness

If you do not solve the problem described above, you may find yourself in the worst pain and the most crippling evil a human being can experience. It is called loneliness. In your feelings, there is a painful awareness that no one cares about you. In your mind and will, you experience a kind of nothingness. Where there should and could be goodness — whether from things or persons — there is nothing. You believe that there is no goodness within you, and that void is more than you can bear. You ache for something or someone to fill you with their goodness. The conscious flow of your being yearns for the comfort of goodness to replace these negative feelings and beliefs.

This loneliness is caused by closing the doors of your heart to others. In doing that you reject the realities that most stimulate your senses, appetites, feelings, mind, and willpower. Only things remain, and they cannot fill you. Once you pursue and possess them they lose their appeal, and you return to your lonely self.

If the loneliness is simply an absence of a meaningful other in the home of a heart that is still looking for the right person, it is a mixed pain or evil. Hope of finding another somewhat relieves the pain and represses the evil.

If the loneliness is the product of hate, of despising people, it is the worst kind. Hate may monopolize your attention for a time, but after a while you will experience only the bitter taste of ashes. Efforts to keep the fire of hate going can be exhausting. And you will find yourself not only lonely but tired.

Is hating always wrong?

To conclude this section on hate we ask a simple question: Is hating always wrong?

Hate that is based on pain relayed to you from your senses, appetites, and feelings is not morally wrong. It is not a sin. It is simply a physical fact being reported by these parts of you. It must pass over and be judged and approved or disapproved by your will before any question of morality or sin enters the picture.

Hate that passes over to your will can be morally permissible or it can be morally wrong.

If the hate is based on a correct judgment about the evil in the other person who inflicts the pain or deprives you of fulfillment, it is not morally wrong. It is good in the sense that it is trying to protect you from being contaminated by the other's evil. It is not wrong to stay away from such a person.

Of course, it would be wrong to hurt another because he or she has hurt you. That should be left to the decision of proper authority. For you to return the hurt is contrary to the best interests of society and your own best interests. By retaliating you lower yourself to the other's level. If you allow hate to build up such a pressure, it can destroy parts of yourself. Revenge ravages not only the other person but yourself as well.

Of course, too, if the hate is based on an insincere or rash judgment about the evil in the other, it is morally wrong to hate and to act on that hatred.

Fear

Very closely related to hate is fear. It is fear that makes you hate or want to close the door of your heart to another.

What is fear? It can be described as a painful feeling brought on by impending danger. It makes you want to run away from or destroy what is frightening you.

Love or reaching out and holding on to things is the first positive force that operates in you. And fear is the first negative force that you experience as a child. It can be operating within you even when you are not aware of it, and there are at least two reasons for this.

The first reason is that you tend to deny its existence. You become edgy and anxious, tense and tight. Hardly able to breathe, you begin to move away from whatever is causing these sensations. Somehow you feel that if you do not acknowledge fear itself, you are all right.

A second reason is that you do not connect fear with embarrassment or shame. "I'm not frightened. I'm embarrassed." But, in reality, over ninety percent of your fears are rooted in embarrassment. You have not lived up to your image or the expectations of others. "What would they think of me if they knew how I acted?" A recording starts to play in your head, repeating over and over that you ought to be ashamed of yourself. And before you know it, your whole nervous system is alerted. When you are in the presence of people who respect you, your first thought is to run away and hide lest they get too close and find out what you are really like. Your embarrassment, then, is actually based on your fear of rejection.

So, whether you do not want to recognize the presence of fear or you are not able to identify embarrassment as a form of fear, you want to avoid anyone who can provoke such ugly feelings within you.

But does fear always act in the way described above?

It can act that way, but it does not have to. It can be one of your best "bodyguards." As hate is meant to help you by nudging you away from pain and evil, fear's first purpose is to alert you to the nearness of the destructive forces that can cause either pain or evil. However, uncontrolled fear can cause you to become unrealistic and neurotic. Such fear has you running away from shadows. This is especially true in today's society with its overemphasis on competition.

One purpose of society is to make it easier to live your life. When you live in community with others you eliminate many of the dangers that you would have to face living alone in a wilderness. But, unfortunately, many in today's world see life only as a game of competition. In this game your worth does not come from you; it comes from your acceptance by others. If you cannot compete, you lose. Under these conditions — unless you are wise — you will lose your worth as a person. You may develop such a sense of inadequacy that your fears overwhelm you like a garden overrun with weeds. To prevent this from happening, recall what we considered in chapter five under the section entitled "Face Your Fears."

So fear, like hate, does not have to be your enemy. God and nature intended it to be a help. Actually, fear is most helpful when it promotes the positive, constructive side of anger, which we will treat next.

Anger

Most people would describe anger as getting upset over something someone has done to hurt them. And it is anger that makes them want to avenge themselves. Obviously, that is a good description, but it shows only anger's negative or destructive side.

The positive side of anger is evident when your charged-up feelings give you such strength that you do not have to run away from the pain or evil. You can stand and hold your ground. You might choose to fight if nothing else can be done; but you do not have to. Fighting might not be the best answer. It could increase the pain and evil you will suffer when the situation is over and you are the lonely winner or loser.

So, anger can be a good friend if you control it and use it wisely. But it can go to excess. It can consume you and destroy another. This is very true when anger is the response to embarrassment. It can strike so fast. You want to wound another as deeply as he or she has wounded you. Perhaps you never thought of it this way, but embarrassment is a destructive force. It points out a fault in you and blots out the perfect picture you have of yourself. A mysterious fear creeps over you. You may even become hysterical. Instantaneously, you hate what that person has done. You want to avenge yourself.

So, while anger can be a good friend giving you strength, it can also become a bully. It can scare you, and it can terrify others. It can be an unruly companion unless you control it and use it to protect love. Then it is precious. It helps you to cope with fear, and it helps you to come to the aid of others as they resist the evil that is threatening them.

You would do well to put your reason in charge of your anger.

Jealousy

Perhaps the most misunderstood negative force you carry within you is jealousy. It is usually described as a desire for what someone else has.

What good purpose did God and nature intend jealousy to serve?

Jealousy is a force within you that prompts you to want the maximum of pleasure and goodness. When you see that another has more you also want more. It is not that you want to deprive the other of what he or she has. You simply want to have it too.

Obviously, to want more pleasure, more goodness, is not a bad thing. It is a good thing. It can prompt you to strive for more. But it can become excessive if it consumes you, makes you resentful, and causes you to take unreasonably from another the object of your desire. In this case it is wrong because it is excessive.

Sadness

So far we have considered hate, fear, anger, and jealousy — forces that prompt you to do something against pain and evil.

We now consider a force that invades you on recognition that nothing positive can be done about a threatening evil. This is sadness. It comes upon you when you have been deprived of pleasure or goodness, and in your helplessness you resort to tears — which may or may not bring relief.

Like loneliness, sadness makes you aware of a certain emptiness. Its pain hurts so much that it seeks comforting relief. Your whole system strives to compensate, but release seems to come mainly through the shedding of tears.

Why this is so we can only conjecture. But it may be because the eyes are so sensitive and are most in touch with what is happening deep within you. Or it may be to make other persons aware of your loss. Even if they cannot help you, their sympathy makes you feel less empty, less alone. But whatever the reasons, tears are the silent language of the broken, hurting heart. They speak a language that even a child can understand.

What can you do about sadness?

Sometimes it is best to do nothing. If your grief is over a real loss, it wants to express itself. It needs a certain period of time to do so.

Sometimes, especially if it is a recurring sadness, it is enough to merely acknowledge it and, then, set it gently aside. Getting busy about your work or trying to think of something pleasant are two good ways to banish this type of sadness.

Sometimes you may have to do something to counteract what is causing your sadness. Its cause may be the fact that you are loving in an immature way or you are loving someone not mature enough to make a return of love. In that case you have to make a choice. If you stop loving him or her, you will be sad; but if you continue in such a relationship, you will be even more sad. You have to measure which is worse and try to live with your decision.

What You Can Do

There are other negative forces within you that react to pain and evil and at a loss of love or a threat to love. They range from disappointment to despair. When your personal goodness and pleasure are attacked they come to your protection. They do not want you to be hurt. Unfortunately, however, they often seek to free you from hurt by drawing you away from others. Then, supposedly, no one can hurt you.

These negative forces can become tenants you would like to evict; but, strangely, you are reluctant to do so. Somehow it seems better to have them than to be utterly alone. Under their influence your love life may take some strange turns. Not to love may be seen as an act of love; and to love may be seen only as an occasion for hurt. Being lonely may then be looked upon as an act of mature self-love — because it keeps a person from being hurt.

In the area of religion, this becomes even more complicated. To some, every form of denial becomes a virtue; and to inflict pain on oneself is seen as an act of love.

Now, since these negative conflicts with love are so much a part of life, you should learn to recognize them and prepare to conquer them. Your purpose will be to replace the negative with the positive.

First, recognize the fact that if others appear to be rejecting you, maybe you are doing the same to them. You may find fault with another's appearance, lack of sensitivity, and way of doing things. Or, you may accept everything about another and do everything for him or her — with the thought in mind that you will be rewarded for having made so many sacrifices. But the other may not even know you put yourself out in this way. All you can see is that the other does not seem to appreciate what you have done, so you feel justified in rejecting him or her.

Second, proceed slowly and cautiously in your efforts to become more positive. These highly charged negative forces are like dynamite that is ready to explode. You will have to tiptoe around them and be gentle with them. As soon as you find yourself becoming excessively negative with another and with life, slow yourself down and treat yourself by doing something you like.

Third, don't be afraid to seek help. You can learn from a positive person how to cope with your life in a realistic, positive way. Such exposure will magnify your negative forces and even cause you embarrassment; but it will help you to see their danger more clearly and make you want to change them.

Summary

The pages of this chapter have described what are called the negative forces of your personality. When they are controlled properly they are the friends of love. But when they grow out of control they are the enemies of love.

The purpose of these forces is to protect you from pain and evil that may arise from a loss of love or a threat to love. They are hate, which may result in loneliness; fear, which is rooted in embarrassment; anger, which may be constructive or destructive; jealousy, which basically is a sign of love but may go to excess; and sadness, which signifies a broken and hurting heart.

All of these forces can aid you in your love life if you control them properly by observing certain precautions.

Marty

In his late forties, Marty has accomplished more goals than most. He won such a name for himself as a successful lawyer that he had little difficulty being elected to his state's senate. When he set his mind to something, he was like a machine. He did not turn off the switch until he achieved his goal.

What was the secret of Marty's drive? His life's history gives us some good indications.

Marty became an orphan at the age of four. Unfortunately, he had to live with a nervous maiden aunt who had neither the experience nor the desire to raise an orphan child. She showed her displeasure often. If Marty was disobedient, he was locked in a dark closet until he screamed he would be good. On such occasions Marty was not sure whom he hated more — his parents for not being there or his aunt who was there. Many a night he cried himself to sleep. Afraid and lonely, he envied other children whose parents were still alive. He promised himself that things would be different when he grew up. He would not be so helpless.

Somehow, despite the many negative forces within him, Marty managed to survive. And he never forgot the promises he had made to himself. He ran his life more on what his mind reasoned to than what his feelings suggested. He was fortunate in that his aunt had kept for him the insurance money derived from the death of his parents. He used the money to go to college and, eventually, to law school.

Why hasn't Marty married? He has told himself that he has not had time for that. That is partly true. But it is closer to the truth to say that he is afraid to open the door of his heart. He is good at loving from a distance, but he is afraid of anything or anyone who approaches him too closely. Some day, he promises himself, he will open himself more fully to love. Knowing how Marty keeps his promises, you can be sure he will.

Questions

1. Why do we have negative forces inside of us? Would we need them if we lived in a world of innocence where no one hurts anyone?

2. What is hate? Is it normal for your feelings to show hate for things and people who cause or occasion pain for you? Is this different from the hate your mind and will have for evil? Do you look on pain as if it were evil? Is all pain evil? Is all evil painful? Is it wrong to hate?

3. Are you familiar with loneliness? Since this is not a perfect world, many people have not matured; but do you nevertheless look for faults in others? Why? Is it to protect yourself? What

does a person have to do to convince you that he or she is worthy of your love?

4. Do a number of things frighten you? How do you react to fear? Do you pretend there is nothing to be afraid of? Do you run away by avoiding what is frightening you? Do you know what constructive anger is? Do you use it to hold your ground and prepare yourself to face the situation?

5. Are you a jealous person? Would it be natural if you were not? How can jealousy help you? How can it hurt you?

6. Do you cry easily? Do you find it difficult to cry? Is there anything wrong with crying?

7. Is religion mostly a negative or a positive experience in your life?

8. Can you keep your negative feelings from becoming excessive by handling them as they occur? Can you cope with them when they show up in another? Do you feel that God and nature were cruel or clever in equipping you with negative forces? Is a rose less attractive because it has thorns? Looking back over your life, would you change your way of acting in this area to some other way? How?

9. What do you think of Marty? His negative drives did help him make and keep the promises he made to himself. With so many negative forces in his life, do you feel they would make him a difficult husband and father?

How Long
Should
Love
Last?

Since much of love consists of moving into and living in another's being, it is normal to expect some kind of permanence. It is natural in making such a big investment to want some kind of guarantee. In this chapter we want to consider how long love should last.

Traditional Viewpoint

For the longest time it was expected that love between human beings — in marriage, within the family, even among friends — would last a lifetime. And between human beings and God it was understood that the love begun in this life would reach its fulfillment in eternity.

Why this need for permanence?

One answer is found in the intensity of love. Love is so charged with emotion that it needs time and space to demonstrate itself properly. This is frustrating. The only relief at hand is to promise that there will be a time, other times, when it can be expressed and enjoyed more fully.

Another answer is found in the depth of love. When love is experienced as a deep uniting force, it also needs time to share itself fully. It is difficult for persons to sustain a deep sharing experience. The physical faculties tire and want relief from such deep uniting. Besides, life — with its more surface demands — needs to be lived. It is only with the promise that there will be time for more and deeper sharing that the disappointment of breaking off such a shared fulfillment is accepted.

For these and other reasons, the dynamics of love need time to be comfortable, to savor and to express each new growth in oneness.

Whether they consciously realized these reasons or not,

people took it for granted that once real love takes root it is there to stay — for a long time, even forever. Fascination might not last, but real love would.

Modern Viewpoint

Rejecting these traditional ideas of love, some moderns have advocated totally different theories about love. They disown the idea of permanence. They claim it stifles love.

According to these new theories, permanence strips away the excitement of newness, and it takes away the challenge of conquest.

It tends to lead people into role playing. Using the terms popularized by practitioners of Transcendental Analysis (see Andrew Costello's *How to Deal with Difficult People*), they act out their roles as child, parent, or adult without actually analyzing their relationships. They remain in the role most comfortable and convenient for them.

It exhausts the originality of sexual encounter. Sex becomes a habit, not an adventure into the unknown expanses of passion and mystery of another's personality.

It ties people down. Even if they have made a mistake, they must live up to the myth that "they have made their bed" and must now "lie in it."

And, in utter defiance of permanent love, they say that love should be spontaneous, uninhibited, experienced as fully as possible each moment and without the delusionary promises of tomorrow or another time. In these atomic times there might not be another time. Love is for now, and it should be without attachments. It should be carefree. Like a cup that is filled, it should spill over on whomever it wills. It should not have to stay stagnant, waiting to be sipped only by someone special. Loving is living, and living comes only one moment at a time. Love, too, should be only for the present moment. Stretching love out to span all time strains it, robbing it of its vitality.

So, they claim, love should be without commitments. It is a gift to be enjoyed here and now — tomorrow is another day. Trying to make it something more destroys it.

A Question of Maturity

Since these old and new ideas are so opposed to each other, can we say that one is right and the other wrong?

Perhaps our best answer should not be based on right and wrong. It should be based on maturity. As we have seen several times in this book, so much depends on growing up or maturing.

Mature love already contains a timeless element. Having weathered the destructive forces that could have torn it apart, it has solidified itself again and again.

Immature love indicates a lack of self-control. Like a young child who knows that restrictions are necessary but still wants to be carefree, it, too, wants a permanence it can count on. However, like a child, it does not want to make a promise of permanence. It is not that stable, that dependable. It still needs to be carefree. To put the burden of permanence on its shoulders is to crush it.

Fortunately, what we now know about children helps us to understand some of this conduct in adults. Those adults who, as children, were not accepted as persons or who did not have enough time to be carefree before restrictions were placed on them now begin to look for acceptance and to regain their lost freedom.

There are many such people in today's society, and that may be the reason why many moderns advocate carefree love. To put any restrictions on love strikes an old nerve and fosters resentment. It can also stir up panic feelings of not knowing how to perform or to please another.

It should be clear, then, that the desire for permanence in love and the actual permanence depend on the maturity of the persons involved.

Marriage Commitment

An obvious example of the necessity of permanent love is the state of marriage.

Marriage vows have always implied that the love given was for a lifetime — "for better, for worse . . . until death do us part." Somehow, it was recognized that marriage should be a stable, lasting relationship. A sexual encounter or a relationship based solely on the attraction of sex was not enough.

There were two good reasons for this.

First, ordinarily, the children of such a union would profit by the secure anchor of permanently united parents. Second, society needs stable families to function properly.

So, it was presumed that when two people were willing to marry, they were ready to commit themselves to a permanent love.

This presumption was based almost entirely on the age of the consenting parties. However, it is now known that mere advancement in physical age is a very poor basis for presuming mental and emotional maturity. Actually, we as human beings experience three different births. There is physical birth, emotional birth which begins around three years of age, and rational or spiritual birth which begins when a child comes to the use of reason. Although these births should follow each other like steps of a ladder, they do not. A person can be developed physically but not emotionally or rationally. If such a person playacts or successfully pretends that he or she is emotionally mature but is not, this will reveal itself at some future date.

A lack of maturity, then, is the reason for the failure of many marriages. And this is why some of them are declared null and void from their very beginning. Such an annulment is entirely different from a divorce. Rather, it is a declaration by the proper authority that an essential element was missing in the original contract. Although there are other instances when these elements are lacking, one important one is concerned with the maturity of the parties involved. The new Code of Canon Law states quite clearly that if for reasons ''of a psychological nature'' a person is ''unable to assume the essential obligations of marriage'' such a one is ''incapable of contracting a valid marriage.'' If, then, in a given marriage this fact is established by proper court procedure, the union is annulled. In other words, the court declares that there was no valid union here from the very beginning.

We see, then, that married love depends very much on the maturity of the two people involved. Without this important element it is impossible to sustain a lasting relationship. Good will, satisfying sexuality, constant need, and dreamy promises are not enough. These can in no way substitute for maturity.

Maturity is a matter of personality development. And this in turn is based on the way we become one within ourselves. We saw this in chapter five when we treated the meaning of true self-love.

Growth in mature love demands constant effort on our part. Mere physical attraction is only the beginning. Further growth is indicated when we discover and learn to appreciate the maturity of the other person. Sheer immaturity dismays us. When the bridge of love is not maturely anchored on both sides it comes tumbling down. If the spans do not meet somewhere in the middle, the structure will snap, and the relationship will cease. And with regret, the more mature person walks away or resigns himself or herself to the reality of another's inability to love maturely.

Achieving Maturity

In our efforts to achieve the maturity that love demands, here are two points to remember.

First, do not confuse maturity with perfection, especially the absolute perfection that training requires of us. No, we are human beings, and an essential part of being human is to be limited. At any one time we can only breathe so much, eat so much, sleep so much, do so much; and, then, we must do these things all over again. It is human to be tired, frightened, and imperfect.

However, it is also human to be honest about our weaknesses and to make a sincere effort to improve our strengths. We hinted at this in the last chapter. If we are truly honest with ourselves, we will recognize our tendencies to act immaturely, and we will set about changing them. That is why Christ could say, " . . . If you live according to my teaching . . . you will know the truth, and the truth will set you free" (John 8:31-32). Unfortunately, because most of us have formed an ideal "image" of ourselves based on our training, we find it very difficult to face up to any imperfections. With such an "image" directing our lives it is all or nothing. We either pretend to be all good or we condemn ourselves for being no good.

So, honesty and maturity are closely related. To have one is to have the other. To have both is to be on the right road to lasting love.

Second, we should keep in mind that exterior closeness or oneness is most rewarding when it is supported by an interior oneness.

To explain: Blossoms on a fruit tree are beautiful in themselves. However, they are most meaningful because of the potential fruit concealed within them. In the same way, kisses and embraces — from the most artless to the most intimate — are beautiful in themselves. However, they are most meaningful when they also express an inner oneness between the two lovers.

Love is a tapestry whose exterior beauty is a result of the intricate interlacing of threads that can be seen only when the tapestry is reversed. What meets the eye is beautiful to behold, but what makes this beauty come alive is the fusion of threads unseen by the viewer. Love is like that: What counts most is the fusion, the union that happens interiorly in the hearts of the lovers.

Once established, this interior uniting is not dependent on youth, external beauty, intense sexuality, popularity, or self-esteem. These aspects are important, but the deeper uniting forces of love must begin to grow for the relationship to survive. Like cut flowers, immature love will die — preserved only as mere petals pressed in the book of memory and time. But if these deeper uniting forces begin to grow, they will provide the basis of a lasting love union.

So, whether love lasts for a short or a long time depends on the quality of love that is shown. And this in turn is determined by the quality of the persons loving. Do they have a mature self-love, that is, are they in control of themselves? If so, are they willing to share themselves? A ''yes'' answer to these questions is the best guarantee of a long-lasting love.

Summary

Here we have examined the traditional and modern viewpoints concerning the permanence of love. Next, we discussed the importance of maturity in answering the question posed by the title of this chapter. Then, we considered why the marriage commitment demands mutual maturity and what happens when it is not present. Finally, we reviewed two ways of achieving the maturity that is absolutely necessary for the attainment of lasting love.

Michael

Michael, age 24, awoke in a miserable mood. From the street below came a blast of honking horns and bickering voices. ''Why can't these Italians be more quiet?'' he muttered. For three years now he had lived in Rome; and it was his custom each morning to look out of his apartment window to observe the sun rising over St. Peter's. Ordinarily, this made him feel privileged to be studying medicine in such a beautiful, historic city.

But today he was angry. He had just received a letter from his girl friend Linda — now his ''ex'' girl friend. She informed him that in a few weeks she was going to marry another man.

He took the letter from his desk. Choking with tears, he read the words, "Mike, you won't believe or accept this, but I still love you. I just can't take your absence anymore. Three years is a long time to wait. I wanted to tell you this when you were in the States for the holidays, but I could not. Forgive me and pray for us."

He wanted to scream, kick, or punch something. He felt betrayed, spiteful, sorry for himself, and guilty. Whose fault was it? Who was to blame? Had it been a mistake to come to Italy to study? She had agreed that it was the right thing to do, hadn't she?

His head was exploding. He had to get out in the open. His room had become a hateful prison.

Almost subconsciously, his footsteps led him to St. Peter's. Looking up, he wondered why things in life could not be as lasting as buildings made of stone. St. Peter's stood there as if it defied time. He stepped inside and poured his heart out before the "Pietá."

After months of agony, he began to think more sensibly about what had happened. Had Linda ever really loved him? He thought of Tennyson's words after his breakup with his lady love. "Can I love her for the love she bore? No, she never loved me truly. Love is love forevermore."

"In some ways it would be easier," he thought, "to say that Linda never really loved me. But I am not sure. I believe she still loves me. Unfortunately, she did not have the capacity to love at a distance. I've had the preoccupations of my studies and exams to fill in the empty spaces of my time. What did she have to fill in the empty places of her loneliness and fears? I know I have loved her; and when this hurt and humiliation passes, I am sure she will always be a special flower in my heart's. garden.

"Lord," he breathed a prayer of resignation, "heal my wounds and help me to learn and mature from all of this."

Questions

1. How long do you feel love should last? What are the reasons why you feel the way you do? Do young people really know what love is? Do older people have an advantage over young people in knowing what love is and how to make it last?

2. Does it seem a lame excuse to trace an instability in love back to childhood and a child's first experiences with love? Do you feel that you had enough ''carefree'' time before your training made you act in a certain way? Do you feel an excessive need to be carefree now?

3. Do you see a great deal of immaturity in the people you know? Do you know when a person is acting maturely or immaturely? Do you feel that on the whole you are mature?

4. Do you agree or disagree with the basic reasons given for seeking an annulment? Why?

5. How does a person achieve maturity? Is it something that just happens, or do you have to learn it step by step? If you do not have anyone to teach you, can you learn it on your own? Do you need the support of others to become mature?

6. To become mature, do you have to be perfect? Why is honesty so important for maturity?

7. Are you an ''exterior'' or an ''interior'' person? To which do you relate better?

8. What do you think about Michael? Who was more to blame for what happened, Michael or Linda? Was either to blame? Do you think Michael's experience with human disappointment will make him a better doctor and better able to deal with the emotional problems of his patients?

10

Jesus:
The
Ultimate
Love
Story

"A picture is worth a thousand words." If that is true, then a picture of Jesus Christ is worth a thousand books. If it is a picture of Jesus Christ as the Man of love, it is worth even more.

It says more to us than the silent sounds of stones, trees, and clouds, and the distinct sounds of birds chirping, water falling, and thunder clapping.

Jesus Christ is the ultimate love story. There is no better way to observe the human heart than to enter fully into his story. Here we will examine his teachings on love for others, love of self, and love of God.

The Setting

If time is defined as a continuous line from a beginning point to a still-to-be-known point, Jesus Christ appeared on that line when society was developed enough to grasp his message of love, sort it out, have time to practice and develop it. (A love so profound needs time to be understood.)

It will help us grasp Christ's message of love if we understand that he came on the scene at a time of dissension. Not only were his people at odds with their Roman conquerors; they were at odds with each other. They desperately needed to cling to something that would unite them. What they chose to cling to were their laws and traditions.

This was a good thing in itself. They were God's chosen people, and their God was vastly superior to the many gods of other religions. To preserve their belief in him by emphasizing his laws was an excellent idea.

In time, however, these laws and the traditions surrounding them became so all-embracing that it caused a separation among the people. Those who knew and scrupulously kept — at least exteriorly — all of the rules considered themselves the salt of the earth; and those who did not do so were considered the scum of the earth.

The parents of Jesus could have been victims of such laws; but, fortunately, they listened to a deeper law within themselves. According to the law, Joseph could have divorced his fiancée Mary because she was pregnant with a child that was not his. He refused to do so.

The birth of Jesus looks romantic on Christmas cards, but a cold cave with only the heat of animals to give it warmth is not a great place to be born. What a discomfort it was for the infant. What an embarrassment it was for the parents.

And, yet, since this is a real love story, in what more challenging a way could the story begin? The oneness of Joseph and Mary with each other and with this Child conceived in such a mysterious way was not weakened by these unconventional circumstances. It was strengthened.

Henceforth, no one would ever be able to point a finger at Jesus and accuse him of not knowing what it was like to be born poor. The rich might accuse him of not knowing what it was like to be born rich and to be unaccustomed to making sacrifices, but not the poor.

Like the first ripples from a pebble tossed in a pond, these first moments of his existence would be the pattern for his whole life. He would thrive on paradoxes: People would have to look beyond mere appearance to observe his stark reality. His words would shock people into recognizing that there was more to life than they were experiencing.

Most would have had difficulty comprehending the poor circumstance of his birth. But, then, they would not understand Calvary's hilltop either.

Obviously, the story of Jesus is not that of an ordinary lover. If we expect the ordinary, we will go away constantly disappointed. If we are open to listen and learn, we might go away confused; but even then we will go away with more than we expected.

His
Message

After a number of quiet years, the time neared for Jesus to engage the noise of the world that fills the ears but dulls the hearts of people. His plan was to preach his message of love to the crowds while concentrating, at the same time, on forming the minds of a chosen few. Day after day, like drop after drop of water, he hoped the wells of their minds would fill with his truths.

Who were these chosen few? Scholars? Politicians? Professional people?

No. They were — in the main — sunbaked, wind-whipped fishermen. He would make them fishers of people. If he could get these hardheaded realists to absorb his teaching, they would find convincing ways of bringing his message to others. But first they had to understand it and make it the fire of their lives. Jesus knew this would not be easy. As with children, the lessons would have to be taught in every tangible way possible and be repeated again and again and again.

Strangely enough, the official inauguration of his mission began at a wedding feast Jesus and his followers were attending. The party ran out of wine. Pleading with her eyes, his mother came to him, hinting that he do something to save the couple and their families from embarrassment. Jesus was reluctant. He was not really ready to launch his mission publicly; but for his mother's sake he consented. When he actually changed ordinary water into choice wine, his followers were amazed. Emotionally aroused, they were now ready to follow him to the end of the earth.

The race had now begun. There could be no turning back.

And what was his overriding message to his disciples and the crowds that followed him? It was one simple word: LOVE.

He spoke of an incredible oneness that human beings have with each other and with God. Somehow the oneness they have with each other determines their oneness with God, and their oneness with God determines their oneness with each other. He emphasized this on the night before he died: "That all may be one as you, Father, are in me, and I in you; I pray that they may be [one] in us . . . " (John 17:21).

Where did Jesus get this special knowledge of love?

It came from his own experience. He spoke from an awareness of his total oneness with God. He was the Son. God was his Father. He was the Father's equal. He spoke of existing before the world came into being. In fact, he supervised its design and its coming into being (see John 1:3). (That part of his message would have to wait until his followers got to know him more deeply; but once that time came, this knowledge would make him the most positive force in their lives.)

For the present, however, he would insist on this one sublime truth: Love is the only worthwhile foundation of all relationships. Might, fear, hatred, anger, and pride do not unite people. Only profound love unites people deeply. He would demonstrate this love continuously. It would cause him a great deal of trouble; and it would eventually lead to his death. That did not matter.

Only love mattered.

Love for Others

Christ was a skilled teacher. He began with simple truths to which everyone could relate. Using these as a foundation, he would go on to deeper realities. And this is exactly the way he taught love.

He knew that most people think of love in terms of reaching out to others or others reaching out to them. Ordinarily, they do not understand love in reference to themselves. Somehow, if they are loving or being loved by others, that makes them feel good. That is enough. Realizing this, Christ spoke only indirectly of a true love of one's self.

Christ therefore began to teach the people to unlock their hearts by loving everyone. It did not matter who the person was. Every person was neighbor to the other. No one should be refused love.

We can imagine how his listeners must have reacted. "What!" they murmured, "you want us to love even our public and personal enemies — even those enemies of religion who are not living up to the laws? We were taught to hate them and stay away from them so we would not be corrupted by them."

We know what Christ said in reply: "Yes. Love them all. Do not do what they do, but love them because of their dignity and heritage. They are children of God, and your heavenly Father cares about them. So should you" (see Matthew 5:45-46).

Christ's answer would need time to settle into their minds and hearts. It would need the loving example of Christ himself toward those who killed him. But, eventually, all would live by the saying: "This is how all will know you for my disciples: by your love for one another" (John 13:35).

Christ was a practical teacher. He discussed not theories but practice. His purpose was to help the minds of his listeners to find a walkable path out of their confusion and darkness.

His teaching was light.

His desired effect was action.

His fundamental principle of love is contained in the words: "Treat others the way you would have them treat you . . . " (Matthew 7:12).

What could be simpler to understand? What could be more down-to-earth? What could be more practical?

He wanted everyone to muffle the sound of "I hate you" with the words "I love you."

For most, this would mean aiding the poor, caring for the sick, visiting prisons, and hearing the cry of all those in need.

For some, it would mean walking the extra mile and turning the other cheek — even more generous ways of offering love.

For everyone, it would mean forgiving the hurts done by others. Forgiveness of enemies is the beginning of love.

Importance of forgiveness

Christ always stressed the importance of forgiveness. He came to forgive people their offenses against his Father. He came to buy them back, to redeem them. And as he forgave, he wanted his followers to forgive.

Why this emphasis on forgiving? Because when people hurt us we instinctively run away or build up a wall to protect ourselves. That is understandable. If we are dealing with physical harm, it is even good. We have an obligation to protect our lives.

However, many of our hurts are not physical. They are emotional. Our pride is hurt; our image is tarnished. We have suffered humiliation, embarrassment. That hurts.

It is here that the practical, psychological genius of Christ shows itself. He knows and wants us to know that these attacks wound deeply only if we let them. That they provoke us is obvious; but, if we learn of him who is "meek and humble of heart," will another's humiliating action really hurt us?

We know who we are, so another's judgment about us does not change us. Why then let another's attack frighten us and fester into unforgivable hatred?

To do so does not make sense. If anything, the other has done us a favor by reminding us of our human limitations. What the other is saying might not be true, but it does point out that we are capable of failing.

Realizing this, we learn to forgive insulting or insensitive remarks; and by doing so we learn to forgive ourselves when we have done the same to another or when we have done something we are ashamed of.

To explain: Most of our inner tension does not come from our struggles with external forces. No, it comes from an over-exaggerated need to perform well in front of others. We do not want to read or sing in public; we do not want to do anything unless we can do it well. We are too frightened to try lest we be laughed at or embarrassed.

Because of this exaggerated need, we all tend to be critical of others when they do not perform well. This invisible wall of embarrassment makes us afraid to get too close to others lest they see something they can criticize in us.

Christ knew of this tendency in us. And he wanted us to be less concerned with our image and more concerned with reaching out to others in love. How he loved Nathanael for his honesty! "This man is a true Israelite. There is no guile in him" (John 1:47).

Forgiving was the remedy that Christ proposed to cure this exaggerated need to measure one's self and everyone else according to an impossible standard.

Forgiving would break down the walls and allow people another opportunity to relate to each other — no matter what they had done or been.

Forgiving would allow all of us to recognize our true stature. It would also make us more loving and lovable.

No exceptions

If Christ wants us to love even our enemies, it is obvious that he wants no exceptions to this rule of love.

According to Christ, all people — the lepers, the mentally unbalanced, the sick, the poor, the sinner — are lovable. The lovableness might be buried deep; but it is there, and we should be on the alert for it.

"But how can I love everyone?" you say. "How many people and how much can one person love? Isn't there a limit to the capacity of the human heart?"

Love can and does embrace the whole world. It excludes no one. But this does not mean that we are going to *like* everything in everyone. It does not mean that we heap fountains of love on someone who presently has only a cup capacity for love.

It does mean that we do not exclude anyone from the circle of our love.

Does this mean we should love everyone equally?

No, it does not mean that. Some are more lovable than others. They can appreciate the pearls of love we are sharing. Others cannot. They need time and space to work out their immaturity. Love is willing to give them that time and space.

So, in practice, the doors of love are to be open to everyone.

Not everyone will want to enter into our lives or allow us to enter into their lives. Love understands. It waits patiently for an occasion to enter. It is even willing to wait for eternity when the heart will have no doors.

If, then, we must love everyone, what about those negative forces we discussed in chapter eight?

The most prominent of these forces is hate, and what we hold concerning it will apply to the others. We know that we are capable of two kinds of hate. It can be in our feelings or in our will. Our feelings of hate turn us away from pain. Our will acts of hate turn us away from evil.

Obviously, Christ was not opposed to feelings of hate. Feelings are never right or wrong. They just are. They are spontaneous, natural reactions to what is pleasing and what is not. Christ showed how he felt about the Pharisees, for example. He could not stand their falseness and how they did everything for show. He called them some terrible, hateful names (see Matthew 23).

What about hate abiding in the will? Will actions are more stable, more deliberate. What does Christ say about such hate?

Assuredly, we may and should make a will act to hate another's wicked actions. But we may not *willfully* hate the person who does the evil.

Christ does not want us to judge or condemn another as evil. First of all, it is not true. The person is still potentially good. Second, it is not our place to make such a judgment. "If you want to avoid judgment, stop passing judgment. Your verdict on others will be the verdict passed on you . . . " (Matthew 7:1-2).

So, Christ teaches us to love others by emphasizing the importance of forgiveness and the necessity of loving everyone without exception.

Love for Self

Christ reminded us of this commandment in Matthew 19:19 when he said, "Love your neighbor as yourself." He obviously meant that we should love others with the same kind of love with which we love ourselves. However, his words have been misinterpreted through the years, and the result is a damaging confusion. Many personalities have been shipwrecked by this misinterpretation.

The causes of this confusion are many. Here are three of them.

First, there is Christ's emphasis on loving others. That seems to get all the attention. Everything is directed toward that.

Second, there is his teaching about denying one's self. "Jesus then said to his disciples: 'If a man wishes to come after me, he must deny his very self, take up his cross, and begin to follow in my footsteps' " (Matthew 16:24).

Third, there is the implicit fear of society against selfishness. Selfishness destroys the very idea of society.

For these and other reasons, many religion teachers have impressed on their students that to think of or to prefer themselves to another is sinful. One such child, when asked what sin is, replied, "Sin is when you do what *you* want to do." He had been given that impression, and he is not the only one who feels that way. The list of possible accusations in this area is a long one. And the precept of their training that most persons seem to remember best is, "Don't be selfish!"

What Christ taught

To understand what Christ actually taught, we will examine various examples of how he made his point.

Notice first the norm that Christ uses for loving others. He says that you should love your neighbor as yourself. If Christ means that loving yourself is hating yourself, then he wants you to love others by hating them. That does not make sense.

So, Christ is very much in favor of loving yourself. He is not in favor of hurting or hating yourself.

How can you hurt or hate yourself? (We ask this in connection with Christ's words that tell you to deny yourself.) Here then are two of the many ways that you can hurt yourself.

One way is to give in automatically to the whims of your senses, appetites, and feelings. What you are choosing is not for your good as a whole person. It is that part of you — your disregarding, irresponsible self — that does not care about what is really good for you that Christ is asking you to deny. And this is why he asks the question, ''What profit would a man show if he were to gain the whole world and destroy himself in the process?'' (Matthew 16:26)

You also hurt yourself by giving in to your prideful self. If you act only for show and to impress others with your ''image,'' you are a very unfortunate person. You will be constantly anxious over the opinion of others. Christ says to you, '' . . . learn from me, for I am gentle and humble of heart . . . '' (Matthew 11:29).

It is these two counterfeit versions of yourself that Christ wants you to deny. When you act solely to satisfy either one of these, you are selfish. You are hurting and hating yourself.

Now Christ, like all good teachers, tells little stories to exemplify what he has taught. Here are three examples.

Of a person preparing to build a tower, Christ said that he should '' . . . first sit down and calculate the outlay . . . for fear of laying the foundation and then not being able to complete the work; for all who saw it would jeer at him, saying, 'That man began to build what he could not finish' '' (Luke 14:28-30).

One of the points that Christ is making here is that you have to love yourself enough to count your personal talents and your material assets before you begin a project. To do so would not evidence pride but, rather, common sense.

A second example is that of a king ''setting out to engage in battle with another king'' (see Luke 14:31-33). What should the king do? He should consider whether he is able with ten thousand men to meet an army with twenty thousand men. If he cannot, he should ask for terms of peace while the other is still at a distance. He might get better terms than if he is invaded.

Again, one of the points that Christ is making here is that it is not evidence of selfishness to face the facts and look out for yourself. If you overextend yourself, you will end up in disaster.

A further example is the story of the ''ten bridesmaids who took their torches and went out to welcome the groom.'' Five of them were foolish and five were sensible. The foolish ones took no oil with them, while the sensible ones did. Since the foolish ones did not bring oil for their torches they had to go out and buy oil. The wise ones refused to give them any of theirs because there would not be enough to go around. (See Matthew 25:1-13.)

In this story, Christ did not insist that the sensible bridesmaids share their oil with the others. No, he commends them for the wisdom they displayed in preparing for the situation.

So, Christ is telling you to be realistic in your love for self. You should not build towers or engage in battles you cannot complete. You must be wise in sizing up a situation.

In more modern terms, Christ is saying that you should *define* yourself accurately: that is, place borders to the picture you have of yourself. To define means to set down the boundaries of something by showing its precise outlines. In defining yourself you do just that. You say that this is what you are capable of. If you go beyond the borders, you are overextending yourself. If you step over into another's life and presume on that person, you are outside your definition. If another does the same to you, he or she is trespassing.

Of course, it is different when you allow another to cross over the borders of your personality because of love. That is not trespassing. That is loving. But even here you are wise if you keep your boundaries in mind. Love, especially the "in love" experience, can make you feel you can handle more than you really are capable of handling. After a while, your torches burn out and everyone depending on you is left in darkness. To give generously but not foolishly is the rule you should keep in mind. But each has to determine that for himself or herself.

Obviously, then, an accurate definition of yourself is essential to self-love. Everyone has a great deal to share. Some may even give their lives for others. Most have to be content with being patient and forgiving.

It should be clear, then, that Christ does not condemn true self-love; he encourages it.

Love for God

In this book we have treated love for others and love for self before considering our love for God. We know that our primary duty is to love God above all. God loved us first, and our first love must be God. But our earliest experience of love comes from our contact with others — the members of our own family.

And from this experience we learn to love ourselves. Only then — as our knowledge of God increases — do we come to recognize him as the source of all love. God's love for us is the reason behind our love for self and others.

After Christ had impressed on his disciples the importance of loving God, like a good teacher he went on to explain why.

First, he taught them that God was their Father (see Matthew 6:9). As the Son of God, of course, God was his Father. But he wanted to show them — and us — that God cared for them as his children. So he taught them to say, "Our Father . . . ." God, then, is not just an impersonal Being but a personal Father who creates us and loves us forever.

Then he revealed to them, gradually, that as the Son of God he was equal to and one with the Father. This was difficult for them to understand. They wanted to, but they did not know how. If only he could show them the Father joined to him, one with him, they would see and accept it. " 'Lord,' Philip said to him, 'show us the Father and that will be enough for us.' 'Philip,' Jesus replied, 'after I have been with you all this time, you still do not know me?

'Whoever has seen me has seen the Father . . . ' " (John 14:8-9).

However, they finally came to understand when they witnessed his death on the Cross. The Father had sent his Son to redeem them and the entire world.

Finally, the truth came clear to them on that first Pentecost after Christ's Resurrection. Jesus had promised that he would send the Spirit-Helper to aid them in spreading the Good News about the redemption of the entire world. (See John 14:16-18,26.) The Paraclete, the Spirit of Truth, would sanctify them and remain with them so that the message of redemption would never cease being broadcast.

Perhaps you never really thought about it in this way, but the whole mystery of God's love for us is contained in the simple sign we make before praying. With the sign of the cross, we do more than profess our belief in the Blessed Trinity. In effect, we are saying: "I, too, love God the Father who created me out of love, God the Son who redeemed me out of love, and God the Holy Spirit who continues to sanctify me out of love."

Thus, it was Christ's revelation about his Father and the Holy Spirit that shed more light on the awesome mystery of God. Until this point in history, knowledge of him was rather vague and impersonal. But with this more personal knowledge of him all can now see him as Creator, Redeemer, and Sanctifier of us all. Now we can relate to him person-to-Person.

The full experience of knowing God personally will have to wait for eternity. Then we will see him face-to-face in what is called the beatific vision. In the meantime, we can establish a personal relationship with God through the three Persons. This is much better than one based on rules and commandments. They have their place, but they were not meant to replace God. We see this when people keep a rule for its own sake rather than as a means of love.

Unfortunately, in the time of Christ, rules had become idols for many of the people. That is why he reminded them that rules were meant to serve people and not the other way around. (See Mark 2:27.) And we today have somewhat the same problem. But if we learn to relate to God personally, we will learn how to keep God's commandments and his rules of love. When we have a close person-to-person relationship with another these rules fall easily into their proper places.

But there is a difficulty here. We all have a tendency to go overboard for material things. We cannot get enough of pleasure, possessions, or power.

The problem is that we seek these material things according to our sense of fairness and unfairness. This would be a decent guide if we acted in moderation or according to right reason. Unfortunately, we do not. As a result, we may want too much because others have too much. We may want to revenge ourselves because another has inflicted harm on us. Consequently, on the basis of fairness and unfairness alone, we can break all the commandments and not feel we have done anything wrong.

When we really overcrowd or compromise our spirit with an excessive pursuit of material things, we leave very little room for another to come and be comfortable within us. We will be constantly pushing him or her aside to make room for more material things. And at the same time we make it difficult for ourselves to enter into another's being. We are too cluttered up with material concerns to be free to love.

It is clear, then, that the purpose of rules and commandments is to keep our inner spirit well-ordered so that we can give and receive love at our full capacity. And this is especially true of our love relationship to God.

Before the time of Christ, most were content to walk in the sight of God. They were happy if God did not turn his back on them. With Christ's coming, however, a new, daring concept of closeness with God is revealed.

Christ promised, ''Anyone who loves me will be true to my word, and my Father will love him; we will come to him and make our dwelling place with him'' (John 14:23). And Saint Paul reminds us that the body ''is a temple of the Holy Spirit'' (1 Corinthians 6:19).

This was an entirely new approach to God. At the burning bush Moses had to remove his sandals because he was in the presence of God (Exodus 3:5). Now, Christ is offering everyone the fulfillment of love's deepest desire — to have the loved one within one's self. And, being a practical man, Christ showed them how. On Easter Eve he passed through the locked doors of the Upper Room, where the disciples were hiding, as if the doors were not there. He and the Father and the Spirit could do the same with our flesh. They can and do dwell within us.

The presence of the Father, the Son, and the Holy Spirit dwelling within us is a perfect example of love's intimate oneness. Their presence within us is the model for our oneness with others.

Unlocking
Your Heart

The ultimate meaning of Christ's life and teaching is that we must love him, others, and ourselves. He says that we must love him above all else and love others as we love ourselves.

That sounds easy; but, as we have seen in this book, loving is not as easy as it looks. Moving into another and receiving another into one's self takes concentrated effort. To unlock the doors of our hearts and to find unlocked doors in another is difficult. And, even if the doors are unlocked, it is not always easy to remove the rubble that has accumulated within. Sensual or emotional gratification can seem more important than truth and goodness. And, besides, it takes a sustained effort to keep the doors of the mind and will open. As John the Baptizer declared in another context: "Every valley shall be filled and every mountain and hill shall be leveled" (Luke 3:5). So it is with love. If we level the hills of pride and fill in the valleys of inferiority, love stands a better chance.

So, the pearl of great price, that Christ says is worth everything else, is love. Paul echoes the Master in his famous passage: " . . . If I speak with human tongues and angelic as well, but do not have love, I am a noisy gong, a clanging cymbal. If I have the gift of prophecy and, with full knowledge, comprehend all mysteries, if I have faith great enough to move mountains, but have not love, I am nothing" (1 Corinthians 13:1-2).

Christ's entire life was an act of love. Although he tried so hard to open our minds to his insights about love, he was mostly concerned that we open our hearts to the full experience of love.

He is that full experience.

He is God's valentine to us.

Loving as he loves, we learn a lasting way to love others. "Love one another. Such as my love has been for you, so must your love be for each other" (John 13:34).

Loving Christ, we love God because Christ is God.

Loving as totally as he loves, we learn a self-love that is total. We learn to love as a whole person, with only one separate part of our personality.

Unquestioningly, you have to experience all of this to be convinced of it. If you have experienced it, you know. If you have not, you can. You can start by clearing away the entrances of your heart. Then you can invite Christ into you.

"But," you may ask, "how do I do this? How do I make contact with Christ?"

There are prayer formulas for making contact with Christ, but the best way is to be bold and invite him in. If he does not seem to be answering your invitation, be patient and keep trying. Actually, he is already there — if you only realized it.

If you make and sustain a living contact with Christ, your steps are leading to lasting love. The road you are on leads to others, to places deep inside of you, and to eternity. There is no better road to travel.

Summary

This concluding chapter tells the story of the undying love that Jesus Christ exhibited to the entire world. It is the ultimate love story, because any love that we have for ourselves and others finds its origin in the life and teaching of Jesus, the Son of God. We learn from him how and why we should love others — by forgiving them and making no exceptions. He teaches us the way in which we must love ourselves. And he stresses the point that the key to all love is the love of God. His message is clear: "Unlock your heart so that you can love God above all else, and your neighbor as you love yourself."

Questions

1. What was the religious scene at the time of Christ? Which prevailed — law or love?

2. What made Jesus such a good teacher of love? Can book knowledge about love equal personal experience? What personal experiences of love did Jesus have?

3. Why is forgiving such a big part of loving others? How is it a surprising gift to the forgiver?

4. Is it possible to love everyone? Can a human heart hold so much love? Must you love everyone equally? Must you love someone who has hurt you? Should you love someone who is no good for you? How can you hate a person's actions or bad qualities without hating the person himself or herself? What do we mean when we say that everyone has a potential for goodness?

5. What did Christ teach about self-love? How can you hurt and hate yourself? What does it mean to define yourself?

6. What was Christ's big secret about the inner life and love of God? What is the purpose of rules or laws in relating to God and others? What does Christ's revelation about God's indwelling mean to you? Does knowing that love is a moving into another's being help you to understand how God can be in your conscious flow, in your being?

Conclusion

This book began on the optimistic note that it had something worthwhile to say about love. Has it lived up to its promise? Has it placed sex in its proper, natural setting as one of many exits from one's self and one of many entrances into another? Has it made you aware of all the doors of love? I hope so.

In concluding this book I want to leave you with some very special truths about love.

First, love is so much more than external attraction.

Second, youth tends to make loving and being loved by others the most important purpose in life. God and self come in second and third.

Third, mature persons begin to realize that love of self determines how one loves and receives the love of others.

Fourth, all the roads of love lead back to Love itself, that is, to God. It might not seem so, but it is true. Even the roads leading away from God are really roads toward him. A person may start out in the wrong direction, but eventually he or she will find that God is at the end of the road.

Fifth, the most important work in life is to unlock the doors of the heart. Locks ensure safety, but after a while they make the heart a prison. To risk the dangers of having a heart without locks is well worth the effort. This does not arise from recklessness. Rather, it comes from a conviction that living is for loving and loving is living.

Before leaving you, I want to thank you for accompanying me on this tour of love. I am sure the reading has not always been smooth. Some of the bumps and potholes you hit along the road are my fault. Some are the fault of love. Love is so big, bursting, and personal it is almost impossible to present it perfectly. Besides, in dealing with the bumps and potholes, you have had to put some effort into grasping the contents of this book. That has helped you make the book your own. My firm hope is that these pages have helped you realize what a beautiful home is your human heart. May this book prompt you to so fill your heart with love that you can place there a sign reading, "No vacancy." Then you will have found the answer to loneliness and to life.

OTHER BOOKS BY RUSSELL ABATA, C.SS.R.

HOW TO DEVELOP A BETTER SELF-IMAGE

A beautiful ''self-help'' book that discusses: the person your training wants you to be, the person your feelings want you to be, and the person God designed you to become. Blends practical psychology with a Christian view of life. **$2.50**

SEXUAL MORALITY: Guidelines for Today's Catholic

A straightforward discussion of sex, giving rights and wrongs and reasons why. Discusses the desire for sex, the relationship between sex and love and the effects of improper sex. **$1.50**

DEALING WITH DEPRESSION: A Whole-Person Approach

A sensible, sympathetic book that considers the roots of depression, discusses unsatisfied needs — social, emotional, physical, and spiritual — and suggests a whole-person approach to overcoming this difficult problem. **$3.50**

OTHER HELPFUL BOOKS FROM LIGUORI PUBLICATIONS

LOVE YOURSELF
by Edward Richardson, M.M.

Shows how you can learn to love yourself without losing the virtues of humility and self-sacrifice. **$1.50**

HOW TO DEAL WITH DIFFICULT PEOPLE
by Andrew Costello, C.SS.R.

Takes a Christian view of communication, expectation, different personality types and ways to improve personal relationships. **$2.95**

Order from your local bookstore or write to:
Liguori Publications, Box 060, Liguori, Missouri 63057
*(Please add 50¢ postage and handling for first item
ordered and 25¢ for each additional item.)*